PRAISE FOR
CAREER 180s

"It takes courage, tenacity, and faith in yourself to make a career shift. It's inspiring to read the stories of those who did just that."

—BEVERLY JOHNSON, SUPERMODEL, FASHION ICON, BUSINESSWOMAN, AND NEW YORK TIMES BEST-SELLING AUTHOR, THE FACE THAT CHANGED IT ALL

"An in-depth look at the soul-searching that comes with making a major professional decision—and the joy and satisfaction of knowing you made the right one."

—HELEN JOHNSON-LEIPOLD, CHAIRMAN AND CEO, JOHNSON OUTDOORS

"This book is very relevant today. I see so many people come back to college to prepare for a new career. It is exciting, and these stories will help show people that is it possible to try something new and to succeed at it."

—DEBORAH L. FORD, CHANCELLOR, UNIVERSITY OF WISCONSIN—PARKSIDE

"Taking a chance and trying a completely new career takes guts. Mike has found a unique set of people that provide inspiration to those who might be considering making a major change in their life's direction."

—JOE SWEENEY, BUSINESSMAN, SPEAKER, AND NEW YORK TIMES BEST-SELLING AUTHOR

T0107152

CAREER
180s™

CAREER
180s™

Inspiring Stories of
BOLD CAREER
CHANGES

MIKE HARRIS

Advantage®

Published by Advantage, Charleston, South Carolina.
Member of Advantage Media Group.

ADVANTAGE is a registered trademark, and the Advantage colophon is a trademark of Advantage Media Group, Inc.

Printed in the United States of America.

ISBN: 978-1-59932-618-4
LCCN: 2016956793

Cover design by George Stevens.

This publication is designed to provide accurate and authoritative information in regard to the subject matter covered. It is sold with the understanding that the publisher is not engaged in rendering legal, accounting, or other professional services. If legal advice or other expert assistance is required, the services of a competent professional person should be sought.

Advantage Media Group is proud to be a part of the Tree Neutral® program. Tree Neutral offsets the number of trees consumed in the production and printing of this book by taking proactive steps such as planting trees in direct proportion to the number of trees used to print books. To learn more about Tree Neutral, please visit **www.treeneutral.com.**

Advantage Media Group is a publisher of business, self-improvement, and professional development books. We help entrepreneurs, business leaders, and professionals share their Stories, Passion, and Knowledge to help others Learn & Grow. Do you have a manuscript or book idea that you would like us to consider for publishing? Please visit **advantagefamily.com** or call **1.866.775.1696.**

To the ten people in this book with the courage, energy, and passion to try something new. The world needs more people like you.

TABLE OF CONTENTS

INTRODUCTION

For most people, change is difficult. We get comfortable with what we know we can do, so most of us keep doing it. It takes a special kind of person to make what I call a career 180: going out on a limb and beginning a totally new professional venture or career after mastering another field.

In this book, you'll find the inspiring stories of ten people who, after reaching the peak of their chosen profession, pivoted to something completely different, people such as Jim Berbee, who built and sold a highly successful IT solutions company and then moved across the country to go to medical school and is now an emergency-room doctor. That's not something very many wealthy entrepreneurs would do. And people such as Anne Reed, a well-known and successful litigator in Milwaukee who gave up her long legal career to run the Wisconsin Humane Society.

I'm glad each of them agreed to tell us their stories firsthand, giving an intimate look at the motivations, challenges, and joys of venturing into the unknown. I also spoke with some of their friends and colleagues to get a better sense of what these professionals' career changes have meant and done for them. I didn't include people whose new careers could be considered hobbies. This book is about people who dove in and gave everything they had to building a new career and, in most cases, developing a new personal brand.

While I was writing this book, someone asked me if any common themes emerged from the ten individual stories. Was there one thing they all did or focused on while deciding to take the plunge? Was there a methodology they generally followed in evaluating the new career path they would take? Happily, the answer is no. These stories illustrate that **there's no one right way to undertake a career 180**. Everyone faced their own questions, challenges, and doubts. Some were quite spontaneous: Roger Brown responded to an ad and soon after found himself as the new president of the Berklee College of Music. Mike Rohrkaste learned of a political opening and decided quickly to run for state office right after retiring from a career in corporate human resources. Others went through years of planning and transition: Wayne Breitbarth slowly ramped up his LinkedIn training and consulting business while he was still a financial executive in the struggling office-furniture industry. He needed to prove to himself that he was good at it, and he certainly is now, as one of the global leaders in teaching LinkedIn skills.

While each career 180 path is different, most of the types of questions here came to mind for the people featured in this book. These are also likely to be questions you'll ask yourself if you are considering making a career 180:

- Why do I want to make this major career change?
- Who will give me candid feedback and advice about making this change? How will that feedback affect my decision?
- Is my family really behind me making this move?
- How will the skills I have built over a lifetime carry over into this new career? Are there any skill gaps I need to fill to be successful?
- Can I handle the new career move financially?
- What will I potentially give up, other than money, if I make this change?
- What will I gain by making this career 180 change?

In many cases, the featured professionals in the book consulted with friends and advisors, while some spoke with a spouse or other family member. In the case of Fran Edwardson, who left United Airlines to run the Red Cross in Chicago, her husband's sudden death was a harsh reminder that life is short, and that gave her the confidence and impetus to pursue a new calling. Sue Ela decided to work with her own family to build a hard-cider company, using the family's historic orchards, after spending thirty years in health care.

Courage, commitment, and willingness to fail were central themes in each of these stories, as well as the feeling that the real risk was in not making the career change. All of these folks expressed excitement, enrichment, and satisfaction from making their career 180s. It sure seems to have worked out well for all ten of them, even though they each had different motivations. Some did it for financial reasons, others because they heard a call, and still others because they had plateaued and needed a new challenge. Robert Finkel had grown disillusioned with the venture-capital industry, so he gave up a lucrative career to open a brewpub in Chicago. Tillie Hidalgo Lima got involved in the family's concierge-services business to return it to profitability and grow the family's wealth. And Connie Duckworth felt a strong need to help the women of Afghanistan find employment and meaning in their lives.

I hope you find inspiration in these personal journeys and, in some small or big way, they help you if you are considering your own career 180. I am always interested in hearing about great career 180s, so if you know of any stories and want to share them with me, visit www.career180s.com to send me a lead. And, of course, if you decide to launch your own new career, I would love to hear about it!

Thanks so much for reading this book. It's been a real pleasure to bring these stories to you. I provided some opening and closing remarks for each story to add some additional context and richness.

Mike Harris
Fall 2016
Milwaukee, Wisconsin

CONNIE DUCKWORTH

Weaving a Better Future for Women

*"The best way to find yourself is to lose yourself
in the service of others."*

Mahatma Gandhi

Connie was a trailblazer who had it all: a big job and a big income with Goldman Sachs. When she decided to leave the corporate world, she didn't know that she would end up dedicating much of her life to improving women's rights and lives in Afghanistan.

With her high energy level and true commitment to women's issues, Connie has created the largest employer of women in Afghanistan. ARZU Studio Hope is a social enterprise created to empower low-income female weavers in rural Afghanistan. The goal is to lift them out of poverty through ethical, artisan-based employment and to offer education and access to health care.

Connie's career transition illustrates how our skills are highly transferable and adaptable to different situations. She used her business and investment background to develop a stable, self-funding enterprise that's changing the lives of Afghan women. While she also serves on boards of impressive corporations such as Northwestern Mutual and Steelcase, ARZU is truly her pride and joy.

ARZU means "hope" in the Afghan language Dari—and this story provides plenty of hope.

This is Connie's career 180 story.

A First for Goldman Sachs

For more than two decades, I worked to shatter the glass ceiling for women across corporate America. Now, I'm fighting for the rights of women halfway across the world.

I was the first female partner and managing director at Goldman Sachs. I mainly focused on fixed-income products, such as municipal bonds, and I worked my way up from institutional sales to managing offices in Chicago, Los Angeles, and New York. It was a great ride, and I learned so much along the way. Needless to say, this kind of executive-level position is stressful and requires long workdays. After more than twenty years in the role, I was ready for a change.

Goals for Retirement

When I retired from Goldman Sachs in 2001, I had a plan. I would spend a third of my time doing corporate work, a third of my time doing charitable work, and a third of my time with my four kids. I worked until the day I gave birth to each one. When I retired, my children were between six and eleven years old, and I really wanted to be more available to them as they entered those all-important middle-school and teen years. The plan was to spend more time on family activities such as school, sports, cooking, and playing.

Soon after I retired, I began serving on three company and three nonprofit boards, and I was spending more time with my family. I felt I was well on my way to achieving my plan.

AN IMPORTANT MISSION

In early 2002, I got a phone call from a friend I've known for many years through the Committee of 200, a membership-based organization of highly successful female entrepreneurs and corporate leaders.

She said, "I put your name in for something interesting. You might get a call." Naturally, I asked what it was all about. She said, "At the direction of President George W. Bush, the State Department is forming a bipartisan commission to help make sure that women have a seat at the table in Afghanistan. It's called the US-Afghan Women's Council. They need a business representative, so I suggested you. I told them you were retired and had a lot of time on your hands."

I actually didn't have a lot of free time, because I was busy with board work, community work, and my kids. But when the State Department called and told me how much the women in Afghanistan needed help, I agreed to get involved. I've always been passionate about women's rights, and I'd spent my whole career helping women make their presence known in the workplace. It seemed like a good use of my abilities. Thanks to an unexpected call from someone in my personal network, I soon became deeply involved with improving women's lives in Afghanistan.

I first visited Kabul, Afghanistan, in January 2003, as one of the business representatives in a US delegation. From my first day there, I could see that real, sustainable jobs for women had to be a top priority if we were going to create lasting change.

Connie (left) thanking one of the weavers.

As I started spending more time on ARZU on top of my various board commitments, my testy teens often pulled my chain. They'd say, not always joking, "Mom, we thought you retired to spend more time with us." It was a balancing act. I made sure that I was available before school and after school until bedtime. I typically worked from 8:00 a.m. to 4:00 p.m., and I could put in a few evening hours, as well. I was able to spend more time with my kids while also setting a good example of working hard for something important.

WEAVING HOPE IN AFGHANISTAN

It took me a year to figure out what sort of business we should start in Afghanistan, incorporate it, receive tax-exempt status, and raise the funding to launch. We wanted to identify and create a true export-quality product with a steady, overseas market. It had to be something that women could make and that people would want to buy at a genuine market price. In Afghan society in 2004, the answer turned out to be hand-woven rugs. Even today, rug-weaving is pretty much the only game in town for the rural women in the areas where ARZU works.

At ARZU, we name each of our rugs and also include the weaver's name so the buyer knows exactly who made it. One of our great rugs is called Forgiveness. One buyer donated his Forgiveness rug to his church, which placed the rug right at the entrance. Now, when parishioners walk in for mass, the rug reminds them to think about whom they should forgive. That's one of my favorite stories.

A Different Philanthropy Model

My strategy with ARZU was to show that a closed fundraising system can succeed. After the initial fundraising, my goal was to make the organization self-sustaining, much like any other start-up I had invested in over the years. We put together seed capital from the US Agency for International Development (USAID). It was a struggle to get that money because we were very different from anything the agency had ever funded. USAID usually offers big block grants to contractors, who then subcontract the work to the point that the money often fails to hit the intended country. We managed to talk them into a very small direct grant for ARZU's first five years.

It took us that many years to develop our footprint. We had to identify the product, find the women to make the rugs, and work with them to get their rugs up to international standards. We also had to reinvent the supply chain completely. The global rug industry is a real horror show of child labor and other abusive labor practices.

The whole point of ARZU is to economically empower women to lift themselves out of poverty, and they have to earn enough to do that. To make sure the women were paid fairly, we had to remove the middlemen from the exploitative supply chain and replace them with ourselves. It wasn't easy, and it took time.

A US start-up typically takes seven to nine years to make money. ARZU is taking a little longer, but we're cautiously optimistic that we'll become profitable soon. That will be my signal to exit my operating-CEO role because then we'll be able to pay someone to do that work. I'll become chairman of the board instead—a transition I look forward to. When I joined the US-Afghan Women's Council and started ARZU, I thought I'd be involved for just a few years. More than a decade later, I'm still running ARZU, and the council still meets regularly.

You Can't Always Plan Your Career

Starting and running ARZU has been a big surprise to me. It certainly wasn't what I thought I'd end up doing after retirement. Although ARZU wasn't in the picture when I first retired, it mushroomed into something that increasingly crowded out my other activities. One of the lessons I have learned from this experience is that opportunity often knocks at really strange times. If I hadn't gotten that phone call, I would have been doing something totally different for the past several years. It might or might not have been equally worthwhile. Try as you might, you can't always plan your career.

The current generation is very socially conscious; a lot of young people want to go into the nonprofit world. I always tell them the same thing: work in the private sector first. The global problems they're interested in solving are vast. All three sectors—private, public, and nonprofit—have to collaborate to get anything to happen. The private sector is going to be the most efficient allocator of resources. Working in the private sector teaches you to solve problems and to think strategically and entrepreneurially. Those skills are often missing from public- and nonprofit-sector approaches. The tool kit you use to address these problems is one you need to acquire before you get involved in the nonprofit or public sector. One of the important lessons I've learned from ARZU is that there are no quick fixes to major problems. You have to celebrate really small victories because that's the only kind you'll get.

ARZU's Success

ARZU began with three rug weavers in June 2004. Twelve years later, we employ about seven hundred Afghans, 95 percent of them women. This number includes rug weavers, peace-cord bracelet makers, and apprentices. The two flagship products are beautiful: hand-knotted rugs, woven by highly skilled artisans, and trendy peace-cord bracelets, woven by older women and unskilled workers. ARZU is now Afghanistan's largest employer of women, and we have sold thousands of rugs.

We go beyond employment to deliver critical services, such as education, maternal support, and clean-water initiatives. The ripple effect of our programs allows ARZU to have a meaningful effect on so many lives. Consider that 70 percent of our weavers now have cell phones, 50 percent own their own homes, and one even bought a car! Our staff in Afghanistan has now grown to about fifty-five people who implement, oversee, and run the daily programs. We hire only local Afghans. We don't bring in expats.

Teaching baking classes in Afghanistan.

These jobs are so important for Afghan women since, most of the time, the resulting income is the only thing that allows them to feed their families or provide them with some level of education. It is truly a way to lift these women out of poverty and hopelessness. I also learned that even with our vast differences in upbringing and surroundings, we share many human values, such as wanting to take care of our family and feel we're contributing.

I get emotional when I think about one young woman who was an ARZU weaver and went on to become the first person from her village to graduate from high school. After graduation, she joined a midwife program. I was fortunate enough to attend a wonderful ceremony at which the village celebrated her, and I was able to see what a role model she was, even for the men of the village. She wrote a beautiful poem about the entire experience. I was so proud of what this woman was able to achieve with the right support.

ARZU has been helping Afghan women for more than ten years. In a place like Afghanistan, that's real longevity. This country has faced so much conflict over the past decade, and the fact that ARZU has thrived in that environment is my proudest achievement. If you're realistic about what you hope to accomplish, you can accomplish great things.

RETIREMENT: A TIME OF OPPORTUNITY

When I retired from Goldman Sachs, I worried, "Will I ever find anything I like doing as much as this? Will I ever have the chance to work with such smart people again?"

As I quickly discovered, that concern was misplaced. The world is full of interesting things to do, and there are lots of smart people. Just about all those with whom I now interact on a daily basis are people I didn't know in my earlier career. They weren't part of my traffic pattern. If I hadn't changed gears, I would never have met these fantastic people and learned so much from them.

My other big concern was that I wouldn't have anything to do. I had this vision of one empty calendar page after another. What would I do with all that time? Again, this concern turned out to be unfounded. As soon as people find out you're retired, you get called for all sorts of things. Can you serve on this committee? Can you join this board? Can you do this? Can you do that?

If I hadn't changed gears, I would never have met these fantastic people and learned so much from them.

Before I left Goldman Sachs, someone gave some good advice: "Don't say yes to anything for a year." Of course, I didn't follow it. When I was asked to do things, I thought, *Sure, why not? It's only one meeting a month or a quarter. Compared with my old schedule, I've got plenty of time.* I said yes to all sorts of things. Then I woke up a year later and found that while I was busy with commitments every single week, they were mostly things I didn't want to do. I wasn't passionate about them. It took another year to extricate myself gracefully from some of those commitments. What I should have said to all those callers was "Thanks for asking. I'm evaluating my choices right now; let me get back to you." That would have let me consciously choose only those things I felt passionately about.

DISCOVERING YOUR NEXT ADVENTURE

I talk a lot with women who, like me, have had long, successful careers and are looking for their next adventure. They all want to stay active and give back. I think it's something in our DNA. Often, as these women conclude the first phase of their careers, they're ready to do something entirely different. Entirely *different* usually means joining a nonprofit, starting a business, or doing philanthropic work and establishing a legacy while continuing the trajectories from their previous careers. I think the key to deciding what your *entirely different* next step will be is finding something that, when you get up every morning, you're as passionate about as possible.

Before making a big career shift, I strongly suggest analyzing the factors you're leaving behind. What do you not want to repeat? What do you want to repeat? What new things do you want to add to your work in your next phase? Some of the women I talk with take their time and look around carefully for their next career. Others just dive into their passions right away. If you follow your passion, the income that might have been a big motivator for you in your previous career could shrink quite a bit or even disappear. In that case, look for an environment that's rich in emotional-fulfillment income instead.

I provide this advice to people who are thinking of a major career switch: Whatever you did in your previous career, you have skills the world desperately needs. Use those skills. Whether it's at the local, national, or international level, it doesn't matter.

> **Whatever you did in your previous career, you have skills the world desperately needs. Use those skills.**

The world has problems that need your intellectual horsepower. Roll up your sleeves and get involved. It almost doesn't matter what you do. You can't make the situation worse, so it only has an upside. It's personally empowering, and it's fun. When you look back a few years later, you may find yourself nowhere near where you might have predicted, but you'll probably be someplace pretty interesting.

Connie's commitment to empowering women everywhere—from the workplace to rural Afghanistan, where poverty runs rampant and opportunities are hard to come by—is truly inspiring. ARZU has brought hope to a nation of oppressed women and serves as a reminder that it's never too late to devote your expertise to a cause that speaks to you.

Connie took the phone call when it came—and she knew pretty quickly that this was the right opportunity for her. It never even crossed her mind that it would turn out to be her life's work. Giving up more than ten years of her professional life for ARZU without any compensation is not something that very many people would do.

By the way, the rugs produced by ARZU are absolutely gorgeous, and I especially love the names that have been given to them. Please take the time to visit the organization's website at www. arzustudiohope.org. It's very well done and exemplifies the quality of the orga-

A Courage rug by ARZU.

nization assembled by Connie and her team.

When I asked Melissa Bertenthal, who has worked at ARZU for many years, how Connie has been able to create something so impressive, she told me, "Connie is an amazing and fearless woman who used her business acumen and personal drive and energy to make a major positive impact on the world." I say the world truly needs more people like Connie.

ANNE REED

It's All about the Animals

"Life opens up opportunities to you, and you either take them or you stay afraid of taking them."

JIM CARREY

Anne Reed spent her entire legal career as a partner at the same Milwaukee law firm, navigating the rough-and-tumble world of litigation. She thought she would end her career at that firm, but an everyday event—researching obedience classes for her dog—presented an opportunity that burrowed itself in her mind.

Once Anne learned of the Wisconsin Humane Society's inspiring and admirable work in her community, she couldn't help but want to get involved. She had doubts about applying for the executive director position, but she kept imagining herself in the role. Her instincts were right: she applied and was offered the position three months later.

Since joining the Wisconsin Humane Society, Anne has expanded the organization's service area significantly, established a leadership mentoring program for employees, and fostered relationships with other organizations to improve the lives of animals across the country. Former board president Tony Enea, who was part of the committee that hired Anne, said it was clear from the start that Anne was "capable of anything she set her mind to."

"Anne has taken the organization to a level that few could have even imagined by leading and mentoring those around her," Tony said. "Anne not only inspires you; she inspires you to inspire others."

This is Anne's career 180 story.

After my first visit to the Wisconsin Humane Society in 1994, I thought I'd never come back. Little did I know that twenty-five years later, I'd be running the organization.

After I married, my husband and I were ready to bring home our first dog. I'd never owned a dog before, and I figured the US Humane Society was where you went to adopt one. I came to the Milwaukee location, and the experience was terrible. The facility was dark, dirty, and noisy, and no one tried to greet or help me. I left with no dog, and my husband and I eventually got our Airedale Terrier, Charlie, from a want ad.

For our next dog, in 2009, I gave the Humane Society another chance. What I discovered was an organization that spoke to me so powerfully that it prompted me to leave behind a thirty-year legal career.

An Honorable Career in Law

I joined Reinhart Boerner Van Deuren, a major Milwaukee law firm, right out of Cornell Law School. In addition to working as a litigator in the courtroom and doing some jury and trial consulting, I was involved in the firm's training programs for young lawyers, mostly focused on litigation.

I always found my work to be very satisfying. My father was a lawyer, and I have always loved the law as a profession and discipline. I was proud and honored to be part of it.

Nonprofit Involvement

As many lawyers are, I was involved in different aspects of nonprofit leadership. I served as the board president of a wonderful organization in Milwaukee called Meta House, which developed innovative and powerful approaches to substance-abuse treatment for women. During my time as board president, we built a strong succession-planning process and a sound board-governance framework. While that might not sound exciting or impactful to most people, I found it really satisfying. Nonprofit leaders and staff do critical work, and the board's job is to support them so they can truly shine. I feel we established a framework for Meta House that prepared the organization for a successful future.

I felt even more connected to the needs of our community through my husband, who has worked for our state public defender's office for many years. In the back of my mind, I always thought my career might include a second chapter where I could give back to the community more directly.

An Opportunity Reveals Itself

After our dog Charlie passed away, my husband and I adopted a new Airedale puppy named Bradley. After my prior experience with the Wisconsin Humane Society, we didn't consider going there to adopt, opting to work with a breeder instead. I was looking for a training class for Bradley, and someone mentioned that the Humane Society had great obedience classes. I visited the group's website to learn more and was surprised and impressed by what I saw. I didn't know that the organization dated back to 1879, or that it advocated for important legislative issues, or that it provided at-risk kids with meaningful educational programs, or that it had moved to a beautiful new facility. I also didn't know it had run a food bank for years for the pets of people in need. I truly had no idea that this organization had such a vast scope and scale, helping ten thousand companion animals and thousands of wild animals every year.

As I looked at the website, I clicked on the page that described the executive director position. The position was open at the time because the previous director had died. Up to that point, I had just been perusing the site, but when I looked at that page, a light bulb came on in my head.

Envisioning a Change

At first glance, the list of qualifications for the executive director position didn't really seem to describe me. The organization was looking for five years of nonprofit leadership experience, and I had only ever worked at my law firm. On top of that, I had no background at all in animal welfare.

That evening, though, my mind kept going back to the job description. As I read through the qualifications again the next day, I had an amazing experience. There's an optical illusion that's a drawing of either a vase or two faces, depending on how you see it. That happened for me with the job description. The words on the qualifications list suddenly turned from not being me at all (two faces) to being exactly me (a vase).

I did have five years of nonprofit leadership experience through my work at Meta House. It was at the board level, which is very different from working as staff, but it was leadership. And as I ticked down the list, I realized I had experience in most of the other skill areas too. Being a litigator gives you a wide range of analytical and problem-solving skills. You have to be a quick study and know how to size people up and gather, master, and present information. You have to communicate well and exude authentic leadership and confidence.

A LEAP OF FAITH

I called a good friend who was on the Wisconsin Humane Society board, and she told me the organization was getting ready to close the search. I had to pull together a résumé almost overnight. Then I started down the hiring path, something I had not done for thirty years.

The process turned out to be more familiar than I thought it would be. Preparing for the interviews with the search committee was a little like preparing for an appellate oral argument in the courtroom. During that process, you think of all the questions the court might conceivably ask you and you write down the answers. I used that technique, and it worked well.

I applied for the job in August, and the Wisconsin Humane Society hired me the third week of November. That's not really very long for a major executive-hiring process, but to me, it seemed an eternity. As the weeks passed, I kept envisioning what it would be like if I actually got the job. Eventually, that vision fleshed itself out enough in my mind that I couldn't help but follow it when the offer finally came.

Announcing the Change

I had been with my law firm for almost thirty years, and I wasn't sure how people would react to me leaving. In fact, they were wonderful. I received so many positive and kind sentiments from so many people. When you work with terrific people for that long, it turns out they truly want the best for you.

On my last day with the firm, a senior colleague told me, "You don't know how to do that." I laugh now because that's probably what a lot of people were thinking, but he actually had the nerve to say it! I can't deny that I had some of those same concerns.

Big Shoes to Fill

My predecessor at the Wisconsin Humane Society, Victoria Wellens, had died of cancer at age fifty-nine. She was widely admired as a leader, innovator, and influencer in the field of animal welfare. Succeeding someone of that stature made my new role more complex. It was critically important to honor Victoria's legacy, and yet any new leader needs to continue to make changes, just as her predecessor would have. It was natural that some people would see my changes as a rejection of something Victoria had done. And since I never knew her personally, it was not possible for me to say what she would have wanted in a particular situation.

In the early days, I relied a lot on people who were familiar with the organization to help me navigate. Instead of suggesting changes on my own, I always sought out others' opinions and made recommendations based on those perspectives. For example, we worked closely with the shelter medicine program at the University of California, Davis and relied on its research on reducing length of stay to improve animal health and outcomes. The program's guidance enabled us to recognize and maximize opportunities to improve our animal care in a way we couldn't have done otherwise. Even now that I have more institutional experience and knowledge, I continue to seek advice from knowledgeable sources when making important recommendations.

OVERCOMING INEXPERIENCE

People often ask me if I miss practicing law. In the early days, I usually said I didn't miss practicing law, but I did miss knowing what I was doing. I didn't have the years of experience I was used to, the experience that enables you to make decisions quickly and confidently.

The biggest gap in my skill set was enterprise leadership. For at least my first two years on the job, if my car were running, I would be listening to an audiobook about leadership and management. I used to joke that I needed a T-shirt that read, "I've never done this before, and I've never seen it done, but I've read about it and I think it's a good idea." I particularly lacked experience in financial decision making, a gap I filled by building a strong team. We have a terrific chief financial officer, and without him, my inexperience on the financial side would be much more evident.

The other key way I've gained knowledge is through my willingness to learn from mentors. Our then board chair met with me every two weeks during the first two years to provide that kind of guidance. I talked a lot with other key board members and with friends who worked at well-run companies. I also met and learned from my counterparts at animal-welfare organizations in other large cities. It was a huge learning curve and one I felt had very high stakes. Failure just wasn't an option.

Something I've learned in this position is that animal-welfare organizations and law firms can both fall into a false tension between creating a supportive workplace and getting the work done. One of the key points stressed by two board members who had both led large businesses was that there is no such tension. A supportive workplace makes it possible to do great work. They shared changes they had made in their own organizations that gave me the courage to pursue this philosophy at the Wisconsin Humane Society.

Leading an entire organization is complicated and difficult, but it's the part of the job I like the best and what I'm most proud of so far.

ADVOCATING FOR ANIMALS

While the Wisconsin Humane Society's status as a 501(c)(3) nonprofit limits how much advocacy work we can do, it's extremely important and rewarding for us to be the mainstream voice for animals. Some animal-welfare organizations only identify with one end of the political spectrum or the other. I feel very strongly that your dog or cat doesn't care how you vote. We need to be the voice for animals, entirely separate from any political partisanship.

Advocacy is one area where my legal skills and experience helped in my new role. As a lawyer, I had to learn new and complex issues quickly and be able to present them with confidence and thoroughness. Advocacy really is the most powerful intersection of my long legal career with my new career.

A COMMITMENT TO RESPECT AND KINDNESS

When I took this role at the Wisconsin Humane Society, I was very inspired by the idea of creating a workplace that was fully consistent with the organization's mission. The US Humane Society values animals and treats them with respect and kindness, and I wanted to exemplify that same level of respect and kindness for our employees.

Since the 1990s, our organization has pioneered techniques that eliminate the euthanasia of healthy, friendly animals for space reasons. When you work with animal shelters, though, death is part of the job, whether it's due to illness or the behavior of animals we don't think we can place safely. It takes a special culture to support and motivate people to do this tough, emotional work, and I feel it is a huge part of my job to foster that culture.

To enhance our workplace, we surveyed employees using an all-staff survey developed by the University of North Carolina specifically for animal shelters, which was extremely helpful in identifying areas for improvement. One of the key changes we've made is establishing a mentoring program for our employees who want to pursue leadership roles within the organization. It's so rewarding to watch our staff thrive as they take on greater responsibility and prepare to lead us into the future.

We've also dramatically increased communication with employees, including all-staff meetings where we discuss animal outcomes and financial results, more discussion with managers to help them better understand their budgets and our results, and restructured teams to foster better communication. These steps may seem basic for many for-profit businesses, but at the Humane Society, as in many nonprofits, they were new and significant.

The people who choose this work are extraordinary. They choose it because they love the mission. I work daily with people who could make more money elsewhere, but they're with us because they care about animals and people. I have to create a workplace they deserve. I want every day here not only to be a day forward for our animals but also a day forward on the career paths of our employees.

Continuous Improvement and Growth

In June 2014, Charity Navigator, America's largest independent charity evaluator, gave us the highest numerical score of any nonprofit organization in Milwaukee. The factors they consider include accountability, transparency, governance, financial health, and management. All of us are very proud of achieving this high rating.

In my time as CEO, we've gone from one location in Milwaukee plus a very small building in neighboring Ozaukee County to four full-scale locations, and we've grown from one hundred employees to 150. Our main, historic location is in Milwaukee, and we've built up the Ozaukee County facility significantly since acquiring it in 2004. In 2013, we acquired the previously separate organization in Racine County, and in 2015, we opened our first spay/neuter clinic, which is open to the public.

Anne cutting the ribbon to open the spay/neuter clinic.

Finding My Stride

They say that if you do something for ten thousand hours, you can master it. I've recently passed the ten-thousand-hour mark at the Humane Society. I don't know if I've mastered the role, but I do answer questions with "I have no idea" less often than I used to.

I've always loved to learn. In this new role, I'm constantly learning so I can better understand our business model and how we generate revenue. I have to make things happen to drive our results. I have been entrusted with 150 jobs and the welfare of twenty-five thousand animals every year. That's a weight and responsibility I never really felt as a lawyer, and I feel honored and deeply satisfied to have this responsibility on my shoulders.

Reflecting on Lessons Learned

If I could do one thing over at this point, it would be bringing the outsourced accounting and bookkeeping in-house sooner. We are an extremely strong organization financially, but we might have avoided some stressful moments if I had added a financial expert to our leadership team earlier.

I never knew my predecessor, but it's easy to see she was a genius with the heart of an entrepreneur. Like many leaders who follow entrepreneurs, I've had to develop systems and processes to set up our organization for long-term success, such as restructuring teams to promote better communication between supervisors and their employees. That's a very common leadership-transition issue, but it was made more difficult by my predecessor's premature death. I feel one part of my role is to enable the organization to operate effectively regardless of who's leading it. Some people are process people. I know I am. I love putting something in place that will work well beyond today. I'm constantly telling our people, "It's good when something good happens, but it's better when we know why." When we're successful because we followed a process, we can achieve success by following the same steps again.

THE VALUE OF NETWORKING

I learned that a strong network is critical when you're thinking about a move like this. Many people, especially those who are younger, have misconceptions about networking. In the early part of my career, I thought networking meant having a lot of shallow conversations and giving people your business card. I was wrong. Networking is about building solid and real relationships in which you're able to help people you respect, and they're able to help you.

I advise young people now to think early about the value of that network and be sure to invest some of their time in it. Building a group of people whose work you know and respect and who know and respect yours will quite possibly be your bridge to your next role when the time comes. Your network will be the people who can fill you in about an organization. Your network will also give you reality checks. They'll be the cautionary voices that say, "Don't forget to ask about this aspect of the organization. Here are possible pitfalls or issues." Most importantly, somebody in your network may tell somebody in that new organization that even though your résumé doesn't look anything like what they thought they were looking for, they should talk to you anyway. That happened to me, and I wouldn't be here without it.

> **Networking is about building solid and real relationships in which you're able to help people you respect, and they're able to help you.**

WORTH THE RISK

People often ask me how the Wisconsin Humane Society found me. I always say they didn't even know they were looking for somebody like me. A lifelong attorney and litigator isn't an obvious choice to lead the Wisconsin Humane Society. In the end, I am so glad our board was willing to take the risk and that I was able to take the risk and leave my comfort zone. I feel blessed to have a job where I make a difference every day and where I can help animals in need and work to make people's lives better too. I am all in with this role. I think of it as my professional legacy. That really matters to me, and it's why I give my heart and soul to this organization.

Anne brings energy, commitment, and high standards to whatever she does, and it's clear she has made a big impact at the Wisconsin Humane Society. Board member Jennifer Bartolotta said, "Anne is a tremendous leader and we are so glad she joined us. She brings us a great balance of stewardship, gravitas, and compassion."

Anne could have easily breezed through her remaining years at the law firm, but instead, she allowed herself to be open and to respond to an unexpected calling. The Wisconsin Humane Society is certainly grateful she did.

Anne told Jennifer that "litigation cannot be what I go out on," and I find that to be such a powerful perspective and emotion. I always say if you cannot sleep at night because of a new possible career opportunity, then it's likely the right opportunity for you. Anne was not looking for a change, but she went for it with gusto once the opportunity materialized. Not everything has to be planned out well in advance. Stay open to the idea of new opportunities that might present themselves in unexpected ways or at unexpected times.

Anne wants to be remembered as a leader who enabled people to thrive and who leaves behind an organizational structure that can sustain success long after her time at the Wisconsin Humane Society. She is proud of what has been accomplished so far under her leadership. I think I can safely say thank you to Anne from all of the animals (and the people) that have been helped by her and her awesome team.

ROGER BROWN

Making Music Happen around the World

"To be prepared is half the victory."

Miguel de Cervantes

Roger is a lifelong learner with a degree in physics from Davidson College and a master's degree from the Yale School of Management. He has an impressive history of philanthropy, having led relief efforts in Southeast Asia and Sudan. He also has achieved remarkable success in business, founding and building the fast-growing company Bright Horizons Family Solutions and eventually taking it public in 2013.

He is a lifelong musician, which makes his decision to lead Berklee College of Music in Boston a perfect story of following one's passion. After his major successes in the business world, he certainly could have rested on his laurels, but he instead chose to assume the demanding role of leading a thriving and growing college.

I met Roger through my son Sam, who is currently a student at Berklee and can personally vouch for Roger's leadership and vision and the quality of what he is doing at the college. The place is literally buzzing with amazing energy, and he has transformed it into a truly global institution.

Here is Roger's career 180 story.

A Lifelong Passion for Education and Music

When I reflect on my life's work, it's pretty clear that I've always been fascinated by and drawn to both education and music. I enjoyed school and went on to teach math abroad and volunteer for both Head Start and the Peace Corps. My love of learning even prompted me to start Bright Horizons, the largest worldwide provider of early childhood education. And I've played drums in rock, gospel, and American roots bands since I was in sixth grade.

One of the things I find interesting about education is the diversity in how people think. My desire to understand how others see the world has inspired me to spend much of my life traveling and working across cultures. When I look at it this way, it seems natural that today I am the president of a world-renowned music college where 35 percent of the student body comprises international students from 105 countries.

Berklee is an amalgam of everything I love. It celebrates music as a way to make the world a better place, regardless of race and social status. It's the kind of school that attracts far more students of color and people from disadvantaged populations than the typical American college. In some ways, my whole life has been a series of tributaries that have led me to this delta where I have the good fortune of guiding an institution full of students and faculty who love and live to make music.

BRIGHT HORIZONS

When I started Bright Horizons in 1986, it was a small team consisting of my wife, Linda, me, and a couple of employees. We had recently returned to the United States after several years of famine-relief work in Sudan for the Save the Children Federation, and we knew we could use our experiences and passion for education to make a difference by providing child care and educational services locally. And we have. By the time I began stepping back from the business in 2003, Bright Horizons had grown to become a public company with seventeen thousand employees and over 750 child-care centers worldwide. We had seven years—twenty-eight consecutive quarters—of reporting earnings growth to the public markets, an achievement of which I am very proud.

As you may know, running a public company can be exciting, stressful, and rewarding, but after seventeen years, it was time for Bright Horizons to have new leadership, and it was time for me to go in another direction. It's just my nature. I have a high need for change and for exploring new possibilities. Unfortunately, while I was ready to make this jump, I wasn't sure where I was going to land. Running a nonprofit or starting a charter school sounded rewarding, especially if it were based in Boston, where my wife and I wanted to put down even deeper roots.

A Letter and a Résumé

With ideas of charter schools driving my day's research, I began reading the trade journal *The Chronicle of Higher Education* because of its cover story about educational assessment. I was so fascinated by the article that I read the journal cover to cover. As I got to the very last page, I saw an advertisement announcing that Berklee College of Music was looking for a new president.

Completely by chance, I stumbled upon the perfect job for me! I felt that my time with Bright Horizons was an experience that would prepare me for a role such as this. As an active musician, I played fifteen to twenty gigs a year. I was even recording children's music for Bright Horizons with an engineer who was a Berklee alum, and whenever I needed another musician, he'd bring in someone from Berklee. I had taken drum lessons from a Berklee professor years before. I not only knew the place; I revered it.

At the time, I had no idea if the college was at the beginning or the end of the search; all I had was the job posting in front of me. I knew enough about executive searches to be aware that people who submit unsolicited applications don't usually get hired, but I contacted the search firm anyway and forwarded a letter and a résumé. Before long, the Berklee Board of Trustees reached out for an interview.

The Search Process

Luckily, I had cut back to working part time at Bright Horizons so I could devote an enormous amount of time to the Berklee search process over the next six months. By the time the interviews came, I likely knew more about the place than my interviewers did. The search committee scheduled an endless number of meetings. One day, I did six one-hour interviews and gave a forty-five-minute speech.

At one of those interview sessions, a faculty member asked me how we could build more of a sense of a community at Berklee. I recognized her from all of the homework I had done, and in my response, I mentioned that I knew she was the director of her church's music group and that she did stand-in gigs in Cambridge.

Her jaw dropped—none of the other faculty members even knew this information.

The homework I completed on the institution as a whole also paid off. My initial assessment of the college, which has proven to be accurate, was that it was a school with an amazing track record that had not been well marketed to the world. Berklee had a huge opportunity to increase the amount of scholarship and financial-aid support offered to attract even better students and improve graduation rates. The college needed to move from an open-admission model to one that was more selective—a change that would actually make more students apply, not fewer.

A Momentous Decision

The engagement process was fun. At Bright Horizons, I had been through many interviews with big clients, such as Cisco Systems, that were selecting a new child-care provider. They always wanted to interview our team, and I enjoyed leading this process. We never knew if we'd win or lose, so we just prepared well and always hoped for the best.

The same attitude and work ethic paid off during the Berklee selection process. I didn't want to adopt the mind-set that I'd been running an organization with seventeen thousand employees and that going to Berklee, which had one thousand employees, would be a step back. I was determined to persuade the search committee members to hire me, instead of putting them in a position to persuade me to take the job. I went all in, which is how I approach most things, and I made my wild enthusiasm about the opportunity very clear.

Hiring a new president was a momentous decision for the board. They reduced the candidates to four semifinalists and narrowed that list down to just two, putting us both through a series of on-campus meetings. Finally, they offered me the job. It was a bit like the days of gladiators. I was the exhausted, proud, victorious one still standing at the end of it.

My wife was thrilled because she knew how perfect the role was going to be for me. We had started a company together and coauthored a book, but it was clear that Berklee wasn't going to hire a couple to be the president. As a classically trained pianist who went to the Rachmaninoff Conservatory in Paris and minored in piano at Cornell, she would have been a great copresident. We were both a little sad that the formal, professional partnership we had had all these years was going to change.

My kids loved the idea. Of all the jobs a grown-up can have, this one, they thought, was really great. My friends and colleagues totally got it and congratulated me on finding such a perfect fit. Of course, many of them wondered if I'd be able to do it or if I'd get started and fall on my face. Believe me, I fought with this fear a little at times. The battlefield is littered with far too many businesspeople who tried to break into higher education and failed.

Looking back, I had no idea this would be the vehicle to my happiness. The things I cared about and wanted to be involved in I've ended up doing here at Berklee. I enjoy international work and learning about different cultures, I love music, I believe in education as the most effective way to change the world, and I see music as the best way to overcome racism and other forms of oppression. Berklee has all of these elements.

WELCOMING NEW CHALLENGES

My previous career taught me a lot, but there were still some gaps in my knowledge. Not everything went smoothly. Working with a faculty union was very new to me. I've never been in a unionized organization before, and as you can probably guess, I researched it extensively before my first day on the job.

I learned that running a college is about supporting and serving the faculty, students, and the board. You have multiple constituencies, and you must respond to all without being beholden to any one or the other. Often, these constituencies will not unanimously agree about change. As another college president pointed out to me, if I were thinking I needed to make a change, I should give my decision six months. I was advised to just listen, observe, and learn. After all, the place had been running for sixty-something years without me, so I shouldn't feel that everything had to happen the first moment I arrived. I knew, however, that when it became obvious a change was needed, I had to present a clear plan and not be timid about it.

Navigating the college's real estate portfolio was also new to me. I'd done a lot of real estate deals at Bright Horizons, but this was very different. Richard Freeland from Northeastern University offered some good advice as we interacted over the years. We often talked about facilities development and how critical it is for cultural change. That was a surprising idea to me at the time, but after facilitating the construction of a wonderful new building for Berklee, I'm convinced he's right. New facilities help symbolize change, growth, and quality to faculty, staff, and students.

We completed Berklee's first building, constructed from the ground up, in the Back Bay area of Boston, a place where land is expensive and hard to come by. All the neighbors felt they had the right to tell us what to do. The city representatives took many opportunities to share their opinions. I had to do a lot of listening, explaining, and learning. I had never really been involved in a world-class architectural design. In fact, I had never paid that much attention to architecture. I decided I should because I was going to be the ultimate decision maker. I didn't want to be the guy who was remembered as building a monstrosity. In the end, the building was a success. It houses 369 student beds, several practice rooms, a cafeteria that doubles as a performance space, and a state-of-the-art recording complex unlike any of its kind. It has won several architectural awards.

Learning from Experience

One of the joys of my job is interacting with the students. In order to get to know as many as I can, I schedule student lunches every couple of months. My office has an open-door policy, and I connect with students and alumni weekly on social media. I routinely invite students to my home for dinner. I recently welcomed a group of nineteen Indian students who helped me to prepare for my most recent trip to India.

To better understand the student perspective, I

Roger addresses a group of Berklee students.

even pretended that I was an entering student early on in my new role, going through orientation, auditioning, and placement exams. I felt it was important to put myself in their shoes, to go through all of the emotions associated with arriving as a first-semester student. I journaled about my experience (now called blogging) and we posted it on our website so students could see what my ensemble rating was (which was reasonably humble). It's been a great tool over the years because entering students read the blog, and it helps them learn what orientation will be like.

Another way I prepared for the role was by asking local college presidents if they'd meet with me to share their thoughts, advice, and wisdom. A funny story one of the presidents told me summed it up perfectly.

He started by telling me that there are three stages of a college presidency. Then he began the story about a new president arriving as the old president is leaving.

"In your desk you'll find three envelopes," the outgoing president says. "Whenever you have a crisis, open the first one and then the second one and then the third one."

It doesn't take long for the new president to have a crisis. He quickly opens the first letter, and it simply reads, "Form a committee." He forms a committee, and everything's fine. Then the next crisis comes, and he opens the second envelope and it says, "Hire a consultant." So he hires a consultant, and everything's fine. When the third crisis comes along, the new president opens the last envelope, and it says, "Prepare three envelopes for your successor."

Do Your Research

I recommend that people who are thinking about changing their trajectory don't immediately go from sixty miles per hour in one direction to seventy miles per hour in a different direction. Give yourself a little break, slow down, and look around a bit. Really think about what motivates you. Otherwise, you could just trade one situation for another and not really be sure it's what you want to do.

By doing your homework, you maximize your chance of success. But more importantly, you'll know whether you want the new role or not. Do thorough intelligence gathering so you understand what you're getting yourself into, and ask important questions that will help you determine whether the role would be a good fit. If you get the job, your research will serve as a foundation for your success.

WORTH THE RISK

I have seen some people who may have left an ideal situation sooner than they should have and never quite found the right next step. And I've seen people who just didn't want to leave where they were because they were afraid to fail in their next role. It can be daunting to go from a current success to something that's risky all over again. But the risks and challenges have been worth it for me.

> Give yourself a little break, slow down, and look around a bit. Really think about what motivates you.

We have experienced great success during my time at Berklee. Our applications have increased by 300 percent. We've gone from admitting about three-quarters of the applicants to fewer than a third. The quality of students is now dramatically better than when I started. Our graduation rates have improved. We have increased our scholarship and financial aid support by more than 300 percent over the past ten years. We introduced minors and master's degree programs, and we opened a campus in Valencia, Spain. Historically, Berklee always produced many fantastic musicians, but now I think the quality goes deeper. The entire student body is extremely talented, which means the faculty members are more enthusiastic because they're teaching stronger students. And with our recent merger with Boston Conservatory, we are now adding award-winning dance and musical-theater programs to the mix. The combined institution is poised to become the world's most comprehensive and dynamic training ground for music, dance, theater, and related professions.

Because this move to Berklee has been so fulfilling, I've encouraged a lot of my friends to at least consider one last big career change. In the end, I played to my strengths, did my homework, and was bold enough to audition for the parts I wanted, and that led me to find my life's harmony and work.

I love how well prepared Roger was for his interviews at Berklee. It showed the board how seriously he was taking this effort. How could they not hire him with his record of success and his preparation? I have been in Roger's Berklee office, which reflects the personality of a guy who loves what he is doing for a living. I also have heard him speak several times, and he communicates in a humble, smart, and visionary way.

Roger had never dealt with the unique world of higher education, including working with a huge board of trustees. But he has done it naturally and very well. He is a great example of having fun doing what you love and still making a huge difference in the lives of countless students and people.

Even as successful as Bright Horizons was, Roger's legacy at Berklee will most likely be his crowning achievement in a very successful working life. Thank you, Roger, for helping so many people to "make the music."

I asked William Holodnak—who was on the committee charged with recruiting a new president for Berklee—why Roger was chosen and how he has done in the role of president. He said it so well that I want to share it with you verbatim:

> The new president had to develop a vision for growth and then execute against that vision, all the while preserving the precious essence of Berklee.
>
> Roger was not produced by the search firm. He responded to an ad in *The Chronicle of Higher Education*, a publication which came to his wife, Linda, at the time a trustee at Yale. He was definitely not looking for a job like this, and Berklee had never imagined a candidate quite like him. He is neither an academic nor an administrator but, rather, a mulligan stew of social entrepreneur, enlightened pragmatist, and aspirational musician. Roger possesses a rare combination of commercial moxie, a sense of mission, and a fatal addiction to jazz and blues. In short, he found us and we found him in a moment of profound serendipity. If I take credit for anything, it was in getting the search committee to wrap its collective mind around an alternative solution and act decisively when someone so unexpected and so appropriate emerged out of nowhere.

I am profoundly gratified by what Roger has been able to accomplish after so agreeably disrupting his great success at Bright Horizons to embrace the opportunity at Berklee. The experiment, in my view, has been an extraordinary success. Berklee is now global, electronic, and ready for anything the future might bring its way.

MIKE ROHRKASTE

Working for a Better Wisconsin

*"Accept challenges so that you may feel the
exhilaration of victory."*

GEORGE PATTON

Mike is the type of person who is always learning and
trying new things. After he decided to retire from a fulfilling career in human resources, he wanted to find a way
to serve his community. He had never planned to run for
political office, but when a few friends told Mike he should
consider campaigning for an open seat in his district, he
started wondering if this might be his next big step. They
all told him to go for it. So he did.

"Mike threw himself headfirst into the campaign
almost overnight," said Tyler Clark, his campaign manager.

"Mike knocked on more than thirteen thousand doors, a humbling experience that he took to right away."

The election became a Rohrkaste family affair, as they all pitched in to help. As a result of their hard work, Mike won his first election and is now dedicating his energy and passion to making Wisconsin's state government work better for his constituents.

This is Mike's career 180 story.

Pursuing the Unknown

"Never take a job where you already know how to do more 20 percent of it." That's the advice one of my mentors, Jack Rhind, gave me early in my career, and the philosophy has stuck with me. Growth doesn't come from doing what you already know; it comes from pursuing the unknown and opening yourself up to new possibilities.

Following that advice throughout my corporate career in human resources led me to take several lateral moves—even going into sales for a while—just so that I could learn new skills. Most recently, that philosophy has led me to another unexpected role: elected official.

Retiring from a Career in Human Resources

I spent the majority of my thirty-two-year corporate career in human resources (HR), the last ten years as an executive vice president and chief administration and HR officer at the Oshkosh Corporation. Oshkosh makes specialty vehicles, including armored defense vehicles, firefighting vehicles, refuse and cement trucks, and construction equipment such as aerial work platforms. I enjoyed working in multiple industries, including manufacturing, financial services, consumer products, and advanced technology. I also had different HR roles, from labor relations to benefits and strategic-acquisition work. Acquisition due diligence and integration were particularly fun and worth the hard work, since they helped us grow Oshkosh Corporation to a company with more than $8 billion in sales.

For the first six years at Oshkosh, I was the number-two HR person, and I moved into the top role when my boss retired. I was honored to help lead a company such as Oshkosh, which has helped to build our country and protects firefighters and those in the military. It was never too hard to get up at 4:00 or 5:00 a.m. to go into work.

Our mission was to provide our customers with the best and safest vehicles and construction equipment possible, and our HR department helped to build a very successful team. The best part of my job and the hardest part of my decision to retire was leaving the people I worked with and knew across the company.

After considerable personal reflection and discussion with my family, I decided to retire in 2014. I had been blessed with a great career but had started to feel my work was becoming redundant. So I told the CEO that I wanted to retire but would stay until the team found a replacement. Once I had made my decision, I started networking to figure out what my next step would be.

I wanted to find a way to give back to our community, as Wisconsin and the Fox Cities area was such a great place for us to raise our family, but I didn't have a plan beyond that. I have served on a couple of nonprofit boards, so I thought maybe I'd explore options such as running a similar organization.

Finding my replacement took a little longer than anticipated. Oshkosh didn't fill my job for several months, and I stayed on afterward as a consultant to help with the transition. By the time I was relieved of my duties, the Wisconsin State Assembly representative in my district, Dean Kaufert, had been elected mayor of the city of Neenah. He had held the assembly seat for twenty-four years, an unusually long time in Wisconsin politics.

POLITICAL CONSIDERATIONS

When I heard the seat was opening up, I didn't think much about it. Then Jim Servi, someone I knew from church, commented that I should run for the position. After that, other people said I ought to consider it too, some jokingly.

While I've always followed politics closely at the national level, I was much less involved in local politics. I hadn't ever thought about running for the Wisconsin State Assembly, but it was an opportunity I might never get again.

I remembered the advice my mentor, Jack Rhind, had given me about being open to new opportunities. Following his philosophy worked out well for me in the private sector, and I think it helped me achieve the top position in my profession. At the same time, even while I kept learning new things up to my last day at Oshkosh, I was very close to burning out by the time I retired. I didn't want to end up like so many people I'd seen before me who had hung around too long and were pushed out or lost their motivation. I knew I was getting close to that point.

So I asked myself if holding an assembly seat was something I could actually do. To answer that question, I used my network. After years of running HR at a Fortune 500 company that was a major employer in the region, I knew a lot of people. I started talking with local business leaders, educators, people at our church, and local officials about the pros and cons of running, what it would cost to run and—most important to me—whether they would support my candidacy. I also talked to US Representative Reid Ribble, a district congressman. Reid's advice was great. He told me what it would take to win with an election strategy, how it might affect my family—good and bad—and that his staff would help me as much as they could.

DECIDING TO RUN

I decided to run because I truly believed I could serve my constituents and help our government operate better, and I knew becoming a Wisconsin State Assembly member was going to require a huge, very challenging learning curve. I've always enjoyed that. What appealed to me most was the chance to learn completely new things in a completely new setting and do some good for my district and Wisconsin at the same time.

I officially retired from Oshkosh on April 30, 2014, and put out a press release a week later, announcing that I was going to run for the 55th District's Wisconsin State Assembly seat. I was on cloud nine that day, even though I was nervous, but the adrenaline of the challenge was all I needed. I was entering a five-person primary race for the Republican nomination. If I won the primary, I had a pretty good shot at winning the seat because the district was majority Republican.

CAMPAIGNS AND ELECTIONS

When I told my family that I was thinking about running for office, they quickly went from surprised to incredibly supportive. Of course, none of us had any idea what it would take to run a campaign. In terms of the physical, mental, and time commitment, it's probably one of the hardest things I've ever done. I shouldn't say, "I," because it was really what we had done. From the day that I announced in early May until the election in November, my whole family was running full speed to win—and campaigning is a grueling process. For months, I was knocking on 75 to 125 doors a day and speaking almost every day at some sort of event or meeting.

My older son, Erik, worked for me all summer during the primary campaign. He and my wife, Debbie, put up signs, helped coordinate events, dropped off literature, and helped with whatever we needed to do. My younger son, Jakob, also pitched in by writing some letters to the editor for me and dropping off literature with his friends. It was a full family affair, and that was a great side benefit to the campaign.

Mike and his son Jakob in the state legislative chamber in Madison, Wisconsin.

I took campaigning seriously and committed a lot of time and resources to the process. I brought in professionals who put together a complete campaign plan that included not just walking door-to-door to introduce myself to voters but also radio advertising and direct-mail pieces. We created a series of events in the district where

I was able to meet with various constituent groups, ranging from recent high school graduates to seniors in assisted-living centers.

I was good at talking with people individually or in groups, but I had never learned how to package my communications into sound bites. Politicians only get about thirty seconds with a person who answers the door and, when you're making a speech, people don't listen to every word, so I hired a public-relations firm to help me polish that skill. I networked quite a bit, which helped me raise money, but mostly, it opened doors and helped me share my position and vision with voters.

THE BEST GUY FOR THE JOB

All of the candidates came from different backgrounds, but we were very similar in our positions on the issues. Because of these similarities, I wasn't sure if I was a better fit for the job than any of the other candidates. At the time, many state issues were related to human-resources issues, such as employment law, unemployment benefits, worker's compensation, training programs, and health care. The more I campaigned, the more convinced I became that my background in HR would be very beneficial in state government. The voters also seemed to recognize that my background would help me understand these issues and make the right decisions. My work in HR had also prepared me to collaborate with other stakeholders on issues, which was appealing to voters.

I was apprehensive, at first, about knocking on doors to meet all kinds of voters. I had more than one run-in with pets. I was bitten by a Rottweiler, but at least the dog's owners voted for me—at least I hope they did! At another house, I saw a dog that looked menacing, so I stopped at the neighbors' house first and asked if they knew him. "Oh, that's Mr. Beans; he's the most gentle dog you can imagine," they said. Sure enough, I visited the house, and Mr. Beans was just as sweet as promised.

Most people were respectful, even if we disagreed, and I encountered only a few rude folks. People gave me water on hot days, offered to pray for me, and engaged with me in many different ways. One interesting conversation that I thought was going well ended when the person I was talking with said, "I'm not voting for you, but I'm sure my husband will." I had many other kinds of great interactions as well. Most people are concerned about jobs, good education for their kids, and making sure politicians spend their money wisely. There isn't as much polarization as the media often lead us to believe.

All of our preparation and hard work paid off. I ended up winning the Republican primary with 32 percent of the vote. The next-closest candidate of the other four had 28 percent. And when the general election came in November, I won my seat with about 57 percent of the vote.

I was glad to win by at least several percentage points above the district Republican-voter enrollment estimates. It meant I was able to carry some independent voters and probably some Democrats, as well. As an HR director, I know a lot about job interviews, and an election is the biggest job interview ever. I had to get fourteen thousand people to say, "Yes, he's the best guy for the job!" I still sometimes wake up and think, *I can't believe I actually won both the primary and the general election.*

Now that I've been elected, I'm proud to serve as someone who understands the value of applying human-resources knowledge to legislation. The other unique thing about me is that I'm not a small-business owner, as most of the legislators are. I had worked at the largest companies in the state. I think that gives me a different perspective on a lot of the issues. It's not better or worse, just different, and diversity of thought is important in state government.

HAPPY TO SERVE

When I started the job, I felt I was back in college, with much to learn. I loved it. I felt completely reenergized and thrilled to be there. Many people who know me well have told me how surprised they were that I got into politics. They also tell me they see a huge change in my enthusiasm and energy level. Politics has rejuvenated me.

One of my jobs as a member of the Wisconsin State Assembly is to sponsor legislation. While it is unusual for a first-term representative to even have one bill become law, I was able to author or coauthor seven pieces of legislation that were signed into law. The laws cover a wide range of issues, including health-care services, job creation, local tourism, and consumer protection. I also successfully included broader pieces of policy legislation regarding rural hospital assistance and drug testing for unemployment benefits and job-retraining programs in the annual state budget that became law.

I attribute a lot of my success in public office to my background in a large corporation. Over the years, I've learned that if you want to get something done, you have to compromise. You also have to develop a plan and focus on what's realistic based on your time and resources. Some legislators want to take on the world, but it's difficult to get things done that way. I've tried to make incremental improvements that are still meaningful to our state and our citizens.

Given my initial success in the budget process and showing an ability to work well with different legislators, the speaker of the Wisconsin State Assembly offered me the opportunity to head a special task force on dementia and Alzheimer's issues in the state. This growing need required legislative changes or funding for caregiver assistance and programs to help patients diagnosed with this incurable and devastating disease. This was a bipartisan project that will have sweeping implications for the future. My mother had dementia in the last few years of her life, and over 110,000 people in Wisconsin have dementia. It is the only top-ten cause of death in America that is on the rise, so it deserves a lot of attention.

The task force resulted in ten bills, three of which became law and provided over a million dollars of funding that will not only help those affected by dementia but will also save the state money in the long run. The Wisconsin branch of the Alzheimer's Association awarded the task force vice chair and me the group's Advocates of the Year award for our work on these issues. I wasn't looking for accolades when I joined the task force, but receiving that award and knowing that we've made a difference in so many lives has been the most memorable experience of my governmental career so far.

Over the years, I've learned that if you want to get something done, you have to compromise. You also have to develop a plan and focus on what's realistic based on your time and resources.

A Wisconsin State Assembly term lasts two years, and I am now running for reelection. I have a Democratic opponent, and I don't plan to take anything for granted. I will continue to work hard to advance key programs to benefit all Wisconsin residents, and my entire family and I are excited about me continuing to serve.

THE LIFE OF A PUBLIC SERVANT

If people were to say to me, "Mike, I'm thinking of doing what you did and running for office or going into public service," I would probably do everything I could do to encourage them. I would want to make sure they realize they're going to be subject to a lot of scrutiny. In public service, your life is always "on." I can't even go to church without somebody asking me a question or bringing up an issue.

I'd also want to make sure they understand that the pay for a public-service position is generally a lot lower than it is for a private-industry position. If you decide to serve, you need to understand the financial hit you might be taking. You also need to understand how time consuming an elected official's work can be. Technically, the legislature in Wisconsin is part time, but the job is really a full-time one and then some. When the legislature is in session, we work fifty- or sixty-hour weeks, or even more. There have been times we were in session for over twenty-four hours straight.

When you're in public service, you get a lot more attention than you did before. You have to be willing to accept that and just get used to it. Running a campaign is very hard—you have to be willing to put the time and effort into it. Still, I would encourage anyone interested in public service to do it.

I think it would be good if more people served in the state legislature for several terms. Most people in the Wisconsin State Assembly only serve for two or three terms. People who stay in office for ten or twenty years, or even longer, can easily become professional politicians. I don't think our Founding Fathers intended people to make lifelong careers out of politics. There's something to be said for people bringing their varied skills to the legislature for a few terms. I don't see myself going beyond three to four terms. By then, though,

I'll understand government a lot better and might decide to stay on or run for something else. Of course, I need to get reelected in 2016 before I can think about that!

I really believe it is best to focus on the skills you need to do something new with your life instead of on your direct knowledge about doing the particular new job. For example, I figured I had good communication and problem-solving skills and I was a good listener with strong relationship building in my past, and that's what a good state legislator has to have. I never let fear or apprehension stand in the way of going for it.

> I really believe it is best to focus on the skills you need to do something new with your life instead of on your direct knowledge about doing the particular new job.

SETTING NEW HIGHS

I thought being the head of HR of a Fortune 500 company was the pinnacle of my career, but so much more awaited me. Holding public office has truly been the highlight of my professional life. At Oshkosh, I made decisions that affected thirteen thousand employees. Now, I make decisions that affect five million residents. It's humbling, exhilarating, and even a little nerve-racking at times. With every decision, I ask myself, *Will this make our state better?* You're not going to please everybody all the time, but I always try to do the right thing for the people of Wisconsin.

Mike's story is inspiring because he took a chance, went all in, and found that he could put a career's worth of knowledge and people skills to good use in a brand-new endeavor. His second career offers Mike the chance to serve, as well as the chance to continue learning new things and solving new problems. His ability to influence voters, fellow legislators, and the governor as a political rookie proves that no matter what your background, if you fully commit to something, engage your network of family and friends, and believe in yourself, your odds of success are high.

Most people just complain about the government and never do anything about it. I respect people like Mike who make the decision to go headlong into politics. It's a demanding and often thankless job. But when people like Mike go into the political arena, I believe it makes the system better and stronger. Maybe we can all coax Mike into running for even higher offices? We sure could use a reasonable and nice guy like this in Washington!

FRANCESCA EDWARDSON

Dealing with Disasters Gracefully

"A happy life consists not in the absence, but in the mastery of hardships."

HELEN KELLER

Fran Edwardson was at what she thought was the peak of her career. As general counsel for United Airlines, she had achieved a longtime career goal and was one of a few top executives at a company with more than one hundred thousand employees. In mid-2003, the new CEO—the fifth in Fran's ten years at United—decided to bring in his former colleague to replace Fran as general counsel.

Recognizing that being ousted under new leadership is a common challenge for executives, Fran left United on good terms. She returned to her former law firm in search of a new type of role that would allow her to lead by influence, rather than position, and empower others.

While exploring some options for her next—and final—career move, Fran learned of a CEO position at the American Red Cross of Chicago & Northern Illinois, where she would be able to give back in a leadership capacity. It seemed like a long shot: the hiring process was already well underway, and she had never worked in the nonprofit sector. But Fran felt a calling, so she moved ahead boldly and used her experience and initiative to prove that she was the best candidate for the role.

Brian Cook was the chair of the Red Cross board search committee that interviewed and hired Fran. He admits that her qualifications weren't an exact fit for the job but said her personal story, resilience, ability to handle pressure, and prior success overshadowed any disparities. He also noted that Fran was "going to something, not away from something," unlike several of the other candidates.

This is Fran's career 180 story.

A String of Tragedies

I'm no stranger to dealing with tragedy.

In June 2001, when I was forty-three, my first husband, Gary Maher, aged forty-five, died suddenly of a coronary aneurysm. We had two sons, Jack, eleven, and Brendan, nine. Overnight, I became a single working mom in a very demanding and stressful executive job, with two boys who needed me to be strong enough to help them cope with their extremely difficult loss.

The experience was a harsh reminder that life is very short. If you want to do something in your life, you really need to get on with it because you don't know how much time you have.

Three months later, while driving to work at United Airlines on September 11, I was listening to *Newsradio 780* in Chicago as two airplanes struck the World Trade Center. We all know the story: terrorists hijacked four planes that morning, including two United aircraft. I had been back at United for only one week since taking time off for bereavement when this unprecedented disaster struck. I remember our CEO, Jim Goodwin, coming to my office that morning. Knowing what I had just been through, he told me I could delegate my role in this tragedy to my team. We knew it was going to be the most chaotic and stressful time imaginable.

While I appreciated his sympathy and understanding of my personal situation, I told him no. I needed to be "all in" or else the terrorists would win—because that's what terrorism is about: causing fear and breaking people. Thankfully, my two sisters jumped in to help with my sons, who were still reeling from the very recent death of their father.

The senior management team at United literally had to pull together to save the company. I have never been prouder of anything than the work that we did in the days and weeks following 9/11. We had to handle a crazy number of complex issues all at once—dealing with labor unions, Congress, the Federal Aviation Administration, Homeland Security, insurance companies, banks, and lawyers—all in the uncertain and scary times after the terrorist attacks. We knew that we needed to be prepared for a bankruptcy filing, and I became the company officer in charge of those arrangements. Very quickly, we had to furlough almost a third of our global workforce. The pace, impact of our decisions, and shifting playing field made this the most intense professional experience any of us had faced. Dealing with the events of 9/11 so closely and personally taught me a lot about what I'm capable of in high-stress situations.

In the year after 9/11, work at United Airlines was very challenging. The terrorist attacks and the company's performance afterward caused us to file for bankruptcy protection in late 2002. By the time the new CEO decided to replace me and several other executives, the job was pretty tough sledding. I actually welcomed the opportunity to leave United amicably and take some time to reflect and reassess where I had been and where I wanted to go next.

TIME TO REFLECT

After leaving United, I took the summer off and then went back to my former law firm as senior counsel. I postponed the decision about whether to return as a full partner while sorting things through. When you're a very senior executive in a large organization like United, you have a lot of people who do your bidding just because you say so. In fact, they often do more than you need because they think that's what you want, and you hold a position of power that impresses or intimidates them.

I wanted to explore leadership by influence, as opposed to leadership by hierarchy or job title, and the law firm allowed me to do that while I formed a clearer picture of my future.

For my next career move, I was considering three options: going back to being general counsel in a large corporation; going back to a law firm to help manage the firm in addition to practicing law; or running a nonprofit organization. My only certainty was that I didn't want to relocate from Chicago, as so many of my family and friends were there. I spent some time with a career coach and investigated all three options simultaneously.

REIMAGINING MY FUTURE

To explore the nonprofit world, I started activating my network. I had been on several boards in the nonprofit sector, so I talked to fellow board members and executives I knew. I learned that, typically, executive recruiters handle filling the CEO position in larger non-profits. The candidates who are considered, however, are often referrals from existing board members or people they know.

One of the people I spoke with, the CEO of a local nonprofit, mentioned that the Red Cross regional CEO was retiring. He forwarded my résumé to another Red Cross executive and, eventually, the recruiter called me.

It turned out that I didn't know any Red Cross board members directly, which was surprising given my strong network in Chicago. Still, several of the directors knew people in common with me, and that really made a world of difference.

After I met with the recruiter for the first time, I had a deeper understanding of the Red Cross's work. It was then that I realized how much it resonated with my personal life. I come from a family that for generations has been very involved in social issues, social change, and giving back. So much so that when I graduated from law school and started my first job at a big law firm, I felt guilty about taking home such a big paycheck. What I realized about the Red Cross job was that I could finally give back in a leadership capacity.

There was another factor, as well.

In learning about the Red Cross's work, I realized that although I wasn't able to save the life of my husband, Gary, here was a chance to help empower other people to save lives. When people face disasters such as we faced at United Airlines, the Red Cross is always there. This job would let me help people in my community, state, country, and even the world. Being able to take my experience and passion and use it for the good of humanity—that resonated very powerfully with me.

THE INTERVIEW PROCESS

By the time I met with the executive recruiter, the Red Cross board already had been through a first round of interviews with several top candidates. Although I was coming in a bit late, I approached the first meeting with the recruiter less as an interview and more for information gathering. I didn't need the job, financially. I wanted to find something that would make me excited to get up in the morning and go to work.

The next step was to meet with the Red Cross board's search committee. They wanted to go through a disaster scenario with me, and while I had great experience from 9/11 and the airline industry in general in disaster planning and response, I lacked specific knowledge of what issues the local Red Cross CEO would face. So, without asking permission, I created my own disaster scenario in a Power-Point slide deck and presented it to the committee in the interview. They were very surprised by my preparation and, afterward, they put a hold on interviewing anyone else for the job. The disaster drills we did regularly at United Airlines really helped me to be prepared and thorough with my thinking and planning.

Taking control of the interview helped me control the vulnerability of my knowledge gaps, but it also demonstrated that I had the skills needed for one the most important parts of the job: disaster response. You need to have your wits about you and be calm, cool, and collected—and planning ahead is critical. Once the hiring process started, it was quick.

BAPTISM BY FIRE

The transition into my position at the Red Cross was also very quick. A few days before I started, the Indian Ocean earthquake and tsunami had wreaked its devastation, and the global Red Cross was in full-blown disaster-response mode. We jumped in immediately to work with local donors who wanted to help.

> Taking control of the interview helped me control the vulnerability of my knowledge gaps, but it also demonstrated that I had the skills needed for one of the most important parts of the job: disaster response.

Less than a year later, after Hurricane Katrina, evacuees from New Orleans and the Gulf Coast began showing up at our offices, looking for help. The first wave consisted of people who had come north to ride out the storm with friends or family and then discovered they could not go home. Many of them were having health issues and running out of money, along with other problems. Our office building became sort of a triage center in those early days, and then we worked with the city of Chicago, United Way, and other agencies and donors to set up multiagency centers to help deal with ongoing issues such as transitional housing, clothes, and schools. Eventually, ten thousand evacuees found their way to the Chicago area from that storm.

A few years later, we helped with the Haiti earthquake relief efforts. We supported evacuees who flew into Chicago with food, temporary shelter, winter clothing, and other needs before they moved on to other points. In an unusual role, we were also involved with the USNS *Comfort*, a navy-owned ship deployed to help handle the numerous surgeries that had to be performed. The Red Cross in Miami recruited two hundred volunteers who spoke Haitian Creole to translate for the injured Haitians, but these volunteers were not equipped to handle the emotional stress of conveying sometimes terrible news to the patients, such as the need to amputate a crushed limb to save the life of a young girl or boy. Our chapter deployed a social worker to lead a mental-health effort to help our volunteers and others involved in the effort deal with these very trying times.

As we responded to these disasters, I knew I was in the right place. Although we were dealing with major catastrophes and personal strife, we were helping people through what was likely one of the worst struggles they would ever face. The work was difficult, but it was immensely satisfying knowing that, together, we were leading initiatives that were bringing people help, comfort, and hope when they needed it most. I knew from personal experience what that need was like.

RIDING OUT CHANGE

The national Red Cross leadership made the decision during the Great Recession to create a shared-services model for handling back-office functions such as accounting, human resources (HR), and information technology (IT). That way, the local chapters could focus on their main priority: service delivery and helping people in need. At the regional level, that meant that instead of having a head of HR, an IT person, and others reporting to me locally, we became customers of the national shared-services group. While I believed the model was the most efficient way to steward our donor dollars, it was a dramatic switch that significantly affected the nature, scope, and responsibilities of my job as CEO.

Frankly, when you see your job change that much, you have to ask yourself if it's still the right position for you. One of the things that really kept me grounded was that when I took this job, I decided it was going to be my last job. I did some real soul-searching but never wavered from that decision. So I had to decide if I would hang in there and support the team through the transition or if I would retire.

I decided to stick with my team, and I'm really glad I did. The job is less complicated and more focused now. While a consistent and repeatable approach across the nation means less discretion over how you conduct your business, the quality of the experience improves for clients, volunteers, and employees alike.

Our influence within the Red Cross on a national scale is stronger too. That's what leadership means to me now—using the power of influence. One example is our national Home Fire Prevention Campaign, which is designed to save lives and is built on local Red Cross programs such as our Team Firestoppers program that started in Chicago. We provide leadership around the national Red Cross system, and I am proud of that.

THE EXPERIENCES THAT LED ME HERE

I truly believe that the different things I've done in my career have all built on each other to prepare me for each of the positions I've held. I took the normal path out of law school and was very grateful to land a job at a wonderful law firm that paid me well. As a transactional lawyer, I learned general business skills, as well as how to think about different kinds of risks and how to allocate them in contracts, which has proved foundational to my work at the Red Cross.

Serving as securities director for the State of Illinois Securities Department in Springfield, Illinois, helped me learn things such as general management skills, politics, media relations, and how to build my network. This period of government service also clarified my career path.

I returned to Chicago from Springfield knowing that I eventually wanted to become a corporate general counsel. I had also learned the quickest path to that role involved becoming a partner in a major law firm. I rejoined my law firm, made partner, and took on internal roles at the firm that helped build my management experience. All these experiences served me well when I left to become deputy general counsel and then general counsel, at United. A year later, I was promoted to senior vice president, became a direct report to the CEO, and sat at the table as part of the senior leadership team.

> **I truly believe that the different things I've done in my career have all built on each other to prepare me for each of the positions I've held.**

The airline industry does a great job with disaster-scenario planning and testing. It's cyclical and hit hard by economic downturns, and it's always in the public eye. We went through a great culture-change experiment during my tenure at United by creating an employee stock-ownership plan in exchange for labor concessions, which ended during United's bankruptcy. These experiences prepared me well for the work I now do in the nonprofit sector.

Obviously, disaster work is core to what I do here at the Red Cross. Economic downturns tend to impact human-services non-profits first with lower donations and greater needs, and we tend to recover last. The shared services and other structural changes we've made at the Red Cross on a national scale that began in the Great

Recession have been accompanied by one of the most dramatic and successful culture changes I've observed in my career.

I believe all these experiences, plus my unsought experience of 9/11, and the experience of my first husband's untimely passing made me an excellent fit for the Red Cross.

WEIGHING THE PROS AND CONS

Being in the disaster-response world means you're often front and center. When bad things happen, people expect you to do good and provide hope. We scale up with people and resources when disasters happen, and the personal demands on your time and energy can take a toll. It's essential to take time for yourself because this can be really hard and draining work. At the same time, being there to help people during a disaster can be very rewarding and gratifying. It's important to remember that no matter how challenging it is, the people we are helping at the Red Cross are going through so much worse. That sense of compassion is critical to performing in demanding times.

Fran in action with Red Cross volunteers.

Another leadership challenge is that you have to get creative about investing in your people and giving them opportunities to grow. As a nonprofit, we don't have the money to enroll them in leadership-development programs or pay for them to get advanced management degrees. We have to find other ways to develop their leadership skills and help them move their careers forward. A big part of my job is to be a coach to the team, mentor them, and build the capacity of the next generation. I enjoy that part of my job and think we've been very creative and resourceful about investing in our people by seeking pro-bono help from our board members and their networks. On the positive side, it's great to see our people flourish when we make these opportunities available to them.

I've learned that every type of work has pros and cons. When people come to me for advice about switching industries or careers, I often ask them, "What is most important to you?" If you are drawn to a type of work because you are passionate about it and instinctively know you'd be great at it, then it's likely that the pros of the industry will outweigh the cons. Sometimes, it takes the loss of a job or another disaster to force you to consider a change, and when it does, it's important to recognize that change—welcomed or not—as an opportunity that can take you where you were meant to be.

There's a lot to learn from Fran's story. First, nothing is guaranteed. Loved ones can be taken from us unexpectedly, as can jobs. Disasters and tragedies can strike at any moment. These are things we cannot control. We can, however, control the way in which we respond to life's unfortunate events. We can get back up, dust ourselves off, and find meaning and inspiration in the things that could have destroyed us or brought us down.

If you, like Fran, have seen your share of tragedies, then you know that it takes strength and bravery to overcome hardship. You also know that what doesn't kill us makes us stronger. In fact, if you look hard enough, you'll often find that the events that have brought you hardship are also preparing you for your next assignment. I love the fact that Fran decided to take a leadership role in helping others deal with disasters. It was the perfect way for her to put professional and personal experiences to work for a great organization.

Fran retired from the Red Cross in January 2016 after leading the organization for eleven years. She made a significant difference in her time at the Red Cross with volunteers, the city of Chicago, local corporations, and the board. What a great way to end a great career. Now, she will serve on various corporate and nonprofit boards. When I asked Fran how she wants to be remembered at the Red Cross, she said, "As a leader who made the place work, created clarity and focus when necessary, was always pushing people to perform at their peak, and helped to develop and teach others." Fran will certainly be a hard act to follow.

WAYNE BREITBARTH

Helping People Link In for Success

"Great things are not done by impulse, but by a series
of small things brought together."

VINCENT VAN GOGH

How could a fifty-something Midwestern CPA become one of the nation's leading authorities on how to use a key social media platform? Only through a destined and deliberate transformation. After putting aside his skepticism and witnessing the power of LinkedIn firsthand, Wayne dove in to learn how to use the social media tool to save his furniture business—but he didn't stop there. Since 2008, Wayne has shared his passion for and knowledge of LinkedIn with over eighty thousand students and professionals across the nation.

Doug Watson, one of Wayne's longtime clients, said Wayne's practical knowledge and approach as a business owner means he understands what clients are trying to accomplish. Wayne's high energy and passion for learning also make his LinkedIn sessions fun.

This is Wayne's career 180 story.

Ups and Downs in the Furniture Industry

I spent a large part of my career—more than twelve years—as the chief financial officer and president/co-owner of M&M Office Interiors. We worked with some of southeastern Wisconsin's largest businesses, but also start-ups and one-office clients, to change, remodel, move, or downsize their interiors. We provided office furniture, movable walls, raised floors, and other products and made sure their spaces fit their needs. Business was good. We were one of the top ten businesses in Waukesha County from 2006 to 2008, and *Inc.* magazine named us one of the five thousand fastest-growing US companies in 2007 and 2008.

Then the Great Recession hit.

Our business dropped by 50 percent almost overnight, so my business partner, Tim Rudd, and I began brainstorming ways to drum up enough business to continue to support our families and put our children through college. It was the second economic downturn in the construction industry—which is closely tied to the office-furniture industry—since we had bought the company in 2002, and tensions were running high.

I stayed in the back office and took care of accounting, so I didn't know much about direct sales. I wasn't on any social media sites such as Facebook, Twitter, or LinkedIn. I was fifty years old and thought social media was for kids. I truly had no interest. A friend of mine, Todd Schwerm, had used LinkedIn to research potential customers and grow his business. Todd was very persistent in telling me that LinkedIn could help us sell more furniture, but I was equally persistent in telling him that LinkedIn was just his new hobby.

MAKING THE CONNECTION

Soon after I had written off Todd's efforts, I was on a business trip to Holland, Michigan, to visit Haworth, our main office-furniture manufacturer. I had some time to kill in the hotel, so I thought, "I'm going to try this stupid LinkedIn thing for twenty minutes." Twenty minutes later, I was amazed.

My first thought was that Milwaukee just got a lot smaller for me because I could see the large network of people I was linked to through my first-degree connections. I'd been working in Milwaukee since graduating from college, so I knew a lot of people, but I didn't know whom they knew. A few clicks on LinkedIn immediately gave me access to that larger network.

Then and there, I ordered a couple of books on LinkedIn from Amazon and studied hard for about two months. Once I felt comfortable with my new knowledge, I asked my business partner if I could set up a meeting with the sales team. He said, "You can schedule any meeting you want, since you own half the company." So I told him, "I've learned how to use LinkedIn, and I want to show everybody else how to do it."

I've discovered that someone in his late fifties can still learn new things, even things that we think only much younger people can understand. I wasn't the most tech-savvy guy, and I knew nothing about social media. Even so, I was able to be relevant and interesting and form a brand around using LinkedIn. Once a skeptic, I'm now a passionate believer and huge proponent.

THE POWER OF SOCIAL

At first, only one of our six salespeople even attempted to use LinkedIn. He was a young guy who liked to socialize and meet people, so I sent him out to all the local networking events, such as chamber of commerce meetings. After each event, he would come back and tell me who was building or remodeling office space and might be a good sales prospect for new office furniture. We would then use LinkedIn to see if I was connected to any of the prospects he was finding. Many times, I did have a relationship with someone at the company and, before we knew it, he and I were doing sales calls together.

Seeing the success that we were having, the other five salespeople started to catch on and use the same process. They also started telling everybody in Milwaukee that their boss had taught them how to use LinkedIn effectively. They'd come back from meetings with clients and prospective clients and say, "This client wants you to teach him LinkedIn. Would you do that?" I said, "Sure. If it's a client, I'll help in any way I can." What a way to differentiate our office-furniture company from all the others!

About three months after I started using LinkedIn, we landed our first sale through the tool. The sale was worth $250,000—a big deal in that economy. I had used LinkedIn to learn that the prospect and I knew some people in common, and making that connection helped us close the sale. I started going on a lot of sales calls with our salespeople because we often discovered beforehand, through LinkedIn, that I had a relationship with someone at the target company.

New Opportunities

I taught 105 LinkedIn classes in my first year, on top of my full-time role as CFO at M&M. The trainings were a great way to interact with potential clients, so my business partner supported my efforts to tell our story in a unique setting. My LinkedIn demonstrations included my profile, so prospects would see our company and my role. Also, I held about half of those meetings in the beautiful conference rooms that we had in our showroom—and you can bet they were loaded with our very best office furniture.

At the end of that first year of teaching, my wife, Brenda, thought we should write a book. It took us a year to write *The Power Formula for LinkedIn Success: Kick-Start Your Business, Brand, and Job Search*. It's now in its third edition. I'm very proud that it has helped tens of thousands of readers to access and experience the full power of LinkedIn.

You'd think that Brenda would be a LinkedIn power user too, but she doesn't even have her own account. She's more focused on working on our business behind the scenes. Brenda edits all my public writing, including my weekly blogs and e-mails, creates all my handouts and other content, coordinates registration for my events, and works closely with my clients on proposals and billing. Her support has been key to my success.

The book has been hugely successful and is one of our most important revenue streams and marketing tools. To date, we've sold more than eighty thousand copies in print and electronically. By the time the book came out in 2011, I had two years of training people in LinkedIn under my belt and was ready to grow that business. My partner at M&M and I agreed to initiate a two-year plan that would transition me from one business to the other.

I slowly reduced my stock in M&M and steadily increased the time I spent training until I was a full-time LinkedIn consultant. By the time I was on my own, my daughters, Erica, Jenna, and Deanna, were finished with college, and the financial pressures that came with that phase of life had passed. My wife and I consciously downsized from a big suburban house to a much smaller house in the city where I could be close to the nonprofits I am involved with. That lowered our expenses enough that I didn't feel I had to make the same amount of money just to feel financially secure. I was ready—mentally and financially—to make a jump.

THE PROS AND CONS OF ENTREPRENEURSHIP

I had several big concerns about leaving the furniture business—and the security of a salary. My entire career had consisted of three jobs, and this wasn't a lateral move. I'd been a business owner, but we had purchased the furniture business, not built it from scratch. And I wasn't sure my accounting experience, though extensive, would help me much as a solo entrepreneur. Health insurance was and still is a concern, but for the time being, I was able to purchase good coverage at a reasonable price. Still, the biggest question was whether LinkedIn would disappear the way MySpace and other once-popular social media platforms had.

Of course, I could also see a lot of advantages to going out on my own. As much as I like being part of a team and leading, I was getting tired of managing people and wanted to control my own schedule. The flexibility was the biggest draw. I'm on the board of three nonprofits—Make a Difference Wisconsin, The Community Warehouse, and a nonprofit I founded, the Urban Promise Lunch Club—and I'm also very active in my church.

With this venture, Brenda and I work more than enough hours, but we don't have to punch a clock and manage people from 9:00 a.m. to 5:00 p.m. Now I can spend time on my nonprofit and church work, and I can travel to Fort Myers to see my granddaughter Luciana Joy and not feel guilty about it. I may not be punching a clock, but I keep very busy preparing for and delivering LinkedIn seminars around the country.

The beauty of being in-demand and self-employed is that I can strive toward whatever income level I want. It's always a balancing act, though. When I get busy producing income, I need to make sure I'm still doing enough marketing. So far, so good. I've been doing enough marketing, even when I'm producing, to keep the ball moving—and the ball's getting bigger every year.

LIVING AND LEARNING

It's been amazing to see how the components of my previous career have prepared me for success, especially when it comes to speaking. Back in my early career as an accountant at Arthur Andersen, I volunteered to teach the new employees and actually received training on how to teach adults. When I was in the car business, I organized our quarterly sales meetings around a theme, prepared all the charts and other visuals, and was always the emcee and one of the presenters.

> The beauty of being in-demand and self-employed is that I can strive toward whatever income level I want.

Probably the most valuable experience was my time as a Sunday school teacher for junior-high kids. For eleven years, once a month,

I taught teenagers who didn't want to be at Sunday school. I would speak for forty-five minutes, and I was good at it; they actually paid attention.

Wayne having fun with his LinkedIn consulting program.

Where I wasn't prepared initially was in marketing my own consulting services. I wasn't good at following up on leads to turn them into sales. I was never an official sales guy; other people did that stuff for me. I didn't know how to write a sales proposal, and I was terrible at following up on the proposals I managed to put together. I never had to draft the wording for a proposal or have that first conversation with clients to try to figure out what their needs were and how my services could meet them. I had approved spending $50,000 a month at some car dealerships on radio ads and billboards and other kinds of marketing, but I never had to do any personal marketing.

I also hadn't developed any one-on-one sales skills. When I began meeting with potential clients, I'd start just telling them what I could do for them instead of listening to them first. To fill in that personal-marketing gap, I worked with Robert Middleton. He specializes in helping what he calls *solopreneurs*, or independent professionals, to learn effective marketing techniques through weekly hour-long tele-seminars. I never missed those sessions. They were incredibly valuable in helping me focus my marketing strategy. I also learned a lot from Michael Hyatt, who teaches personal development, leadership, pro-ductivity, and developing your personal platform. He helped me fill in big gaps in my understanding of online business marketing.

By working on my marketing and sales skills, I've built a solid clientele that continues to grow. My customers mainly come from my public-speaking events, e-mail marketing, referrals, and, of course, from LinkedIn and other social media channels.

A Gradual Approach to Transition

I was very fortunate to be able to transition into self-employment gradually. Having the safety net of staying at the office-furniture company part time while I was launching my LinkedIn career was critical to my success. I have the temperament of a CPA, meaning I'm a conservative, cautious guy. Quitting suddenly would not have worked for me.

If you're thinking of quitting your job and doing something else, try doing it on the side for a while first. If the new work stays fun and interesting, then explore it some more. As long as you have a job, I wouldn't recommend you just quit it unless it's just killing you to still be there. Try to launch your new career quietly.

A great opportunity is out there for all of us, but not every opportunity is great. You've got to do your homework. Try to get close to people who are already doing what you'd like to do. See if they'll spend some time with you, or follow them online or take their training.

The first year I gave LinkedIn seminars, I spoke for free most of the time. I was still working in the office-furniture business, so I could present these sessions free of charge while I got to know the ropes. Before I could quit my day job, I needed to know if I was a good speaker, if I had a good topic, and if people liked me. Without all those free talks, I might not have figured that out. I think you have to wade out into the water a little bit first, see if it's fun, and see if people tell you you're good at it before you really launch.

> A great opportunity is out there for all of us, but not every opportunity is great. You've got to do your homework.

When you're pushing sixty years of age, you don't have a lot of shots left for changes. If you make a commitment to yourself—*Okay, in the next three years, I'm going to try to do this one thing*—and it doesn't work out because you haven't done your due diligence, then what? You might not have another chance. With the right preparation, though, you may find yourself in a better place.

Wayne's story shows us that when we open our minds to learn something new, amazing things can happen. He works for himself now and loves the freedom he has with his work schedule at this stage in his life. Wayne is a hard-working guy and he is not slowing down, but this career change lowered his stress level and put him directly in charge of his own destiny—and income.

Wayne was in the unique situation to be able to test his new career in teaching LinkedIn without giving up his steady job in the office-furniture business. That may not work for everyone, but it is an unusual and interesting way to approach a major career change.

Wayne has had a big impact on helping many companies improve their results by using LinkedIn. His strong financial and business background has really been the perfect basis and complement to his approach of helping many people understand the benefits of using LinkedIn.

TILLIE HIDALGO LIMA

Rebuilding the Family Business

"Faith is a place of mystery, where we find the courage to believe in what we cannot see and the strength to let go of our fear of uncertainty."

BRENÉ BROWN

After committing to a career in pharmacy, one doesn't often end up running a concierge service for businesses—and being very good at it. But that's what happened with Tillie.

Tillie took over as CEO of her family's business under stressful financial conditions, motivating her to become involved in the Cincinnati business community and to seek advice and coaching from local business leaders. Her hard work and willingness to adapt and ask for help transformed her from an inexperienced CEO to a leading female executive mentor. I believe everybody in Cincinnati knows Tillie!

Tillie is smart, fearless, and driven, and she is highly committed to quality, integrity, and transparency. She turned out to be a natural leader and role model, and we are all glad she was able to use those excellent skills and instincts to create jobs and grow a company. I am sure her former pharmacy customers would be proud (and not at all surprised) by what Tillie has accomplished at Best Upon Request.

This is Tillie's career 180 story.

EARLY LESSONS IN PERSEVERANCE

My family escaped from Cuba with a suitcase and ten pesos when I was an infant. I'm the only one of my parents' six kids who was born in Cuba; the others came after we moved to Atlanta and began living in one of the first US housing projects. Despite our circumstances, my parents were amazing role models. I learned a lot about perseverance and courage from watching them face the everyday challenges of being in a new country. We spoke only Spanish at home, so I went to kindergarten not knowing a word of English. My teacher thought I was deaf and asked my mom and dad to take me to the doctor to get my hearing checked. Back then, they didn't have English as a Second Language programs. If only my kindergarten teacher could see me now!

Education is so important to Cuban families. My parents taught us that no one could ever take away our education. Because my dad's job as a chemical engineer with Procter & Gamble took us from Atlanta to Cincinnati, my siblings and I attended parochial grade schools and private Catholic high schools. My parents saw this as an investment during our formative years for a foundation of Christian leadership and academic excellence.

I attended the University of Cincinnati (UC) as an honor student and received a scholarship to the College of Pharmacy. I had always wanted a career that would allow me to serve others. I considered being a pediatrician originally, but I wanted to be a mom and have a career that wouldn't take away too much time from my family. My mom suggested I become a pharmacist, just like my grandfather, Francisco Hidalgo. I loved math, science, and working with people; it was the perfect fit. Plus, it paid well enough to work part time while raising my children.

I met my husband when I was eighteen, and we married when I was twenty-one and he was twenty-two. Our first goal in marriage was to finish college. Two years later, in 1983, I graduated from UC.

I practiced as a pharmacist for thirteen years, starting in an inner-city, community health center. Then I went to work for a small, family-owned pharmacy close to my home in the suburbs. I loved it. I knew the name of every single person who walked into the store. I felt I was connecting with people's lives and understanding their needs. My role was much more than what I learned in pharmacy school; it was an opportunity to be a positive influence in our customers' lives.

An Idea Is Born

By 1992, my husband, Dave, and I had three daughters, ranging from two to eight years old. Dave was working in business development for an architectural engineering and design firm, and he noticed that many of the companies he worked with were seeking ways to create a more productive and enjoyable work environment by offering unique benefits that would attract the best employees.

After talking with his sister, who worked as a concierge in a large office building, Dave came up with the idea of offering concierge services—combining convenience services, such as dry-cleaning pickup and selling stamps, with errand running—to businesses as an employee benefit. I thought it was a great idea for him to pursue, but, even though we had always talked about working together, I wasn't ready to leave my pharmacy job to join him. I had already shelved the idea of attending business school to focus on my pharmacy education and my family.

Dave launched Best Upon Request in 1993, acquiring the contracts from an original entity founded in 1989. It quickly became a success, and by 1996, Dave needed help. Over dinner one night, he asked me, "Do you know someone who is really good with numbers and great with people?" And he sort of wink-winked at me. I said, "Dave, you can't afford me."

BAPTISM BY FIRE

I loved being a pharmacist, but I was ready for a change. I had gotten tired of standing behind a counter and counting out pills. It was killing my knees! And I couldn't even go to the bathroom without someone knocking on the door to tell me a doctor was on the phone for me. When my husband asked me to come work with him, I accepted the challenge and saw it as a chance to try something new.

I told him, "Don't forget, I'm not the wife who comes in to decorate the office." When he told me that he wanted me to focus on special projects, I replied, "How about if I run the operations? I know how because I've managed a pharmacy." He agreed, and I became vice president of operations, which was a real baptism by fire.

During my first few months, I relied on what I already knew from running the pharmacy. When dispensing prescriptions, quality is imperative. You have to get it right every time because a mistake can, literally, kill someone. I was vigilant about accuracy, even when it came to putting the labels on the pill bottles. A creased label could lead customers to think our pharmacy work was careless. My motto is, "How you do one thing is how you do everything." I brought that same approach to Best Upon Request and got the operations to focus on quality and service excellence.

When our president resigned three years later, I took on that role too. I had proved myself to Dave, and he had confidence in me. So I embraced the added responsibility even though I still had a lot to learn. Dave and I worked well together; our styles were very different, yet complementary. I took things on and figured everything out by just doing it.

LEARNING HOW TO SWIM (AND HOW TO ASK FOR HELP)

In 2000, we lost a major client that represented 74 percent of our revenue, with only a sixty-day notice. Consequently, we struggled financially. Then 9/11 happened and we lost even more clients; it nearly devastated us. Shortly after, my mammogram came back positive for possible breast cancer. It was a very hard time, financially and emotionally. Fortunately, a biopsy showed I didn't have breast cancer, and Dave was able to secure a Small Business Administration disaster-recovery loan for us, with our house put up as collateral.

By 2002, Dave was feeling burned out by the challenges of the business. In April of that year, Dave called me into his office to tell me that either I needed to lay off two employees or that he needed to go. I was shocked and, before I could reply, he said it was time for him to find another source of income for our family, and that I was ready to be the CEO. The first thing that came to mind was my fear of networking and becoming the face of the company, which held me back at the time. Today people laugh when I share this because I'm now known as the queen of networking and enjoy connecting with people.

During my transition to CEO, Dave explained the dire financial situation of the company. I knew things were bad, but I hadn't realized that we were on the brink of bankruptcy. The first month I was officially president and CEO, I received a call from our banker inquiring about our line of credit. He said, "I'd like to see the AR." I said, "When would you like it by?" I hung up the phone, called my accountant, and asked, "What's an AR?" I learned it meant accounts receivable, or money owed to us by our clients. By making time to learn and apply business fundamentals, we've come a long way and are now in a strong financial position by all measures. The company has been profitable since I became CEO and became debt-free in 2012. Today my banker shares our turnaround story to inspire other business owners who are struggling.

One of my first goals as CEO was to get Best Upon Request certified as a minority business enterprise (MBE). I learned a lot about the elements of a successful business by going through that process, such as the importance of having positive cash flow, staying on top of AR, and being financially strong so corporations will see you as an attractive, low-risk supplier.

After Best Upon Request became a certified MBE, I received a scholarship for an intensive, weeklong program at Kellogg School of Management at Northwestern University, and later at Tuck School of Business at Dartmouth, to learn how to build a high-performing minority business. I learned how important networking is and about other aspects of building and leading a business.

What helped me get through my time as a new CEO was that I was willing to learn and to ask for help. I joined Vistage International, an executive coaching organization that provides leadership training and business coaching to CEOs. Thanks to Dave's introduction, I engaged with a very talented local business coach and Vistage chair, Jean Lauterbach. In 2005, I created a board of advisors at Best Upon Request because I wanted to be surrounded by thought leaders who would help me understand what I didn't know and where to focus my efforts to generate success.

My advice to any business executive is to seek learning opportunities and coaching because knowledge is power. The courses at Kellogg and Tuck were difficult but so eye-opening because they allowed us to compare benchmarks with other successful companies. Having a board of advisors gave me confidence and increased my decision-making power to execute on our strategy. As a result, we entered into a period of 40 percent growth from 2005 to 2008.

> **My advice to any business executive is to seek learning opportunities and coaching because knowledge is power.**

Strengthening the Family Business

When I started working at Best Upon Request, our kids were still in elementary school. They started working at the company after high school, when they were teenagers. Now, two of my daughters work in the business with me. Jessi is our vice president of marketing communications and Natalie is our human resources leader. We were the first mother-daughter team to go through the Next Generation Institute at the University of Cincinnati School of Business's renowned Goering Center for Family and Private Business. Before us, it was usually fathers with sons and just a few fathers with daughters. We were also the first Hispanic business to complete the program.

Natalie Lima Hall, Tillie Hidalgo Lima, and Jessi Lima Bollin (photo credit: *Cincinnati Enquirer*, 2013).

My girls don't see themselves as working for their mom. We work as a team alongside each other. Still, sometimes, one of them will come to me with a question, and I'll say, "Do you want my answer as your CEO or do you want my answer as your mom?" Or they'll preface their query with, "Okay, I'm asking you as my mom." Even Jessi's five-year-old daughter Grace loves coming into the office and talks about joining the company one day. I love the fact that my granddaughter has strong female leaders as role models.

We recently published an article in our internal employee newsletter highlighting several sets of family members who work together, in addition to our family. My daughters were quoted in the story, and they explain our dynamic best:

"I get to see my mom and sister almost every day," shared Jessi Lima Bollin. "We are very honest with each other. It works for us because we know our boundaries and recognize when we are talking to each other as family members versus our business selves. We put the needs of the business first. BEST is a business family before a family business."

Natalie Lima Hall shared, "The best part of sharing Best Upon Request with my mom and sister is that we can all share something in common. We are all extremely invested and committed to Best Upon Request, and so our conversations around strategy and culture always are rewarding and impactful. It's energizing sharing a passion with someone you are so close with!"

MEANINGFUL CONTRIBUTIONS

Today, we serve customers in nineteen states, plus Puerto Rico, and have 112 employees.

Because I am a Hispanic female business leader, I feel that it is important to spend time talking with community groups about my background. I am an active member of the Cincinnati area community, serving on the United Way board of directors, the St. Elizabeth Healthcare Board of Trustees, and I have served previously on other boards.

I spend a lot of time mentoring people, mostly young women. I love looking for rising stars in the minority community and giving them a lift. Being so involved with the community takes time away from the company, but I've discovered that it can also generate business. It's very worthwhile.

Serving on boards is very important to me because I feel very strongly that they need women, especially minority women, to broaden their horizons. Diversity of thought and diversity of background is critical for board members. The proof is in the data: A McKinsey & Company study found that companies with more ethnic diversity and more women on their boards are financially stronger.[1]

Tillie working closely with her daughter Jessi (photo credit: AP, 2014).

1 Vivian Hunt, Dennis Layton, and Sara Prince, "Why Diversity Matters," McKinsey & Company, January 2015 http://www.mckinsey.com/business-functions/organization/our-insights/why-diversity-matters.

ADVICE FOR THOSE CONSIDERING A CAREER TRANSITION

If I were doing it all again, I would find a business coach earlier in the process to help me with my business acumen and to navigate the challenges of work-life integration as a working mother. It wasn't easy to become the CEO while my family expected that I would still make dinner every night. My husband and I eventually worked out a shift in our professional roles, but it wasn't easy. When you have a challenge, get comfortable calling someone up who has been through it before to ask them, "How did you deal with this?"

Also, focus on what matters most to you. I live out my values every day, which are called the seven Fs. I learned the first five from my parents: faith, family, friends, freedom, and fun. Later, I added two more: fitness and finances. My values serve as my compass in everything that I do because values dictate behaviors, which create successful performance in every aspect of life.

Finally, be courageous. Courage is like a muscle: the more you use it, the stronger and better it gets. Look for opportunities to step out of your comfort zone and try something new. Find a great mentor and follow your passion.

Tillie had a lot to learn when she joined and took over her struggling family business as a first-time CEO, and also, it was her first experience in the world of business. She stepped up when things were difficult. She turned things around and grew the company to become very successful. Best Upon Request is now a thriving family business, with two of Tillie's daughters also managing the company and expecting to take on more responsibilities when ready.

Family is obviously very important to Tillie, and that weaves itself through her entire life story.

Another telling and impactful part of Tillie's personal story is her family's escape from Cuba when she was just an infant. They settled in Atlanta and lived in one of the first housing projects in the United States. She encountered language barriers on her first day of kindergarten and overcame them without the help of established programs, which shows that she forged her extraordinary determination, perseverance, and courage at a very young age.

And she gives back all the time by serving on boards and providing introductions and networking help to many people.

JIM BERBEE

Life in the Emergency Room

*"That some achieve great success is proof to all that
others can achieve it as well."*

Abraham Lincoln

Jim Berbee was the epitome of a successful entrepreneur. He started, built, and sold his company—and made
a lot of money in the process. Unlike most people who
achieve this dream, Jim didn't head to the beach, play
golf all day, or otherwise goof off. He decided to enroll in
medical school and become an emergency-room physician.

There is so much to love about this amazing story. I
love Jim's desire to take on a huge and difficult challenge
and to focus on the emergency department (ED), a part of
the health-care system that is very stressful and intense. I
believe some of Jim's desire for challenge stems from his

entrepreneurial and competitive personality. Jim has also been able to use his well-honed sales and communications skills from his business career to build rapport quickly with ED patients.

The sacrifice Jim and his wife Karen made by moving from their lifelong home during his medical education is also impressive. I suspect many people would not have made and stuck with the commitment to go back to school for nine years to be able to work in the ED. Jim took all of this on once he had earned complete financial security with no need to ever work again, which tells me a lot about his character.

Paul Shain, a longtime friend of Jim and the CEO of Jim's former company, says, "Jim embraces every activity he undertakes with a passion and focus that is unwavering. His ability to channel energy in such a complete and effective way is a skill and trait I have never seen in another human being."

This is Jim's career 180 story.

SELLING SUCCESS

In the fall of 2006, after more than a decade of work, I sold my company based in Madison, Wisconsin, Berbee Information Networks Corporation (Berbee), to CDW, a large public company based in Chicago. Several factors prompted my decision to sell. The economy was doing well, the company was doing very well, and it was time for our investors to see a return on their money and for me to do something else. I was forty-two years old.

I've always liked to start things and watch them grow, but I have less enthusiasm for day-to-day management. I thank providence every day that Paul Shain was the CEO of Berbee. He is an extraordinary individual. As an executive, he brings a magic combination of strategic thinking, commitment to execution, and kindness. Without the strong partnership we enjoyed, the company would never have been so successful.

By the time of the sale, I had become interested in going to medical school. People often ask me if it was something I had always wanted to do. The answer is no. I never had a strong interest in medicine. My father was a professor of forestry at the University of Wisconsin and my mother was a researcher. Medicine wasn't on my radar when I was growing up.

A Budding Interest

I crashed my bike—okay, I fell off it—while I was training for an Ironman race and wound up in the emergency center with a broken collarbone. The entire experience, from how things were run to the care I received, impressed me and gave me a small window of insight into emergency care. I wasn't sure what I was going to do after I sold the company; I was forty years old then and didn't know what to do next. Medicine was an intriguing option.

My wife, Karen Walsh, and I were planning to start a foundation that would focus on human health and welfare. We saw our success as an opportunity to give back, and we wanted to do something meaningful that would make a difference. Medicine certainly fit those goals, and I knew that becoming a doctor would help me with the foundation by exposing me to the needs of the medical community firsthand. Also, my entrepreneurial streak meant that I still wanted to invest in business, and medicine and health care offered a lot of opportunities.

Medicine became my career choice because it was the trifecta: I could actively help people; I could see what the problems were from a philanthropic perspective; and I could see what the opportunities were from a business perspective.

MANDATORY PREREQUISITES

My approach to getting into medical school shows both my ignorance and my arrogance. I was pretty well-known in Madison, Wisconsin, and I was on the board of the University of Wisconsin Foundation. I figured I'd just visit one of the deans of admissions at the University of Wisconsin School of Medicine and Public Health, who'd say, "Oh, great! When do you want to start?" Instead, the dean said, "Well, here are all the things you're going to have to do." That included all the science courses any premed student has to take, along with taking the Medical College Admission Test (MCAT). This is a challenging examination of problem solving, critical thinking, and science knowledge. If you want to get into med school, a good score on the MCAT is essential.

That deflated my balloon a little bit. After some consideration, I realized if I were going to become a physician, there would be many obstacles in my path. Nothing easy is ever worthwhile. To fulfill the prerequisites, I went back and spent the better part of two years as a student just to consider taking the MCAT and applying to medical school. I was trained as an engineer, so I had all the math and physics courses, but I didn't have the chemistry and biology background. I went back as a "special student."

My "special-student" years were some of my favorites. As luck would have it, my niece, Caitie, was also attending the University of

Wisconsin Madison as an undergraduate in education. We would meet on Fridays between classes, and she often brought me chocolate chip cookies. I treasure that time.

MEDICAL SCHOOL

I started thinking about medical school in 2005, and it took two years to finish the prerequisite courses. We sold Berbee in the fall of 2006, and I was accepted to Stanford in 2007. I thought being a student again might be difficult; I was twice the age of the typical medical student and accustomed to navigating my own course. To my surprise, taking direction from younger people wasn't a problem at all. Medicine is hierarchical, but it's a hierarchy based on knowledge and experience. Years matter, of course, but the years translate into knowledge and experience.

In medical school, you have so much to learn that you welcome anybody who can teach you something. My classmates were really wonderful, even though I was old enough to be their father. In fact, I was often compared to some random father of different classmates. I always took this as a nice compliment. They were inclusive; they invited me to all their events, including their keggers. Occasionally, I would go, even though the party would start after 9:00 p.m., and that was my bedtime.

Medical school was a great experience even though I struggled initially with establishing a new learning process. As an engineer, I would solve problems by starting with fundamentals and working from there. Engineering is easy in that sense. If you know the fundamentals and the equations, you can break down the problem and everything falls into place. Medicine isn't so simple.

What made it so difficult for me was that medical school takes a lot of raw memorization, especially in the first years. It felt as if I were memorizing nothing but weird, unrelated facts, but my class-mates with backgrounds in life sciences didn't seem to have as much trouble putting the pieces together. I didn't have a framework to hang everything on. That was humbling and frustrating. There is also no doubt in my mind that learning becomes more difficult with age. All I could do was hope that a pattern would eventually emerge, and eventually, it did.

Jim Berbee, flight physician, UW MedFlight.

THE PRICE OF COMMITMENT

I've lived in Madison my whole life. My parents still live in the same house where I grew up. I had never lived more than two or three miles away from the hospital where I was born. So when Karen and I picked up and moved to California for four years, I promised her that we'd come back to Madison when medical school was over.

Part of the reason for the move to California was to establish a "line in the sand." I wanted to send a clear signal that my business career was before and my medical career is now. I think if I had stayed in Madison for medical school, I would have been constantly pulled into distractions from my previous life. I realized that to make the 180-degree change I was contemplating, I would have to give it my entire focus. For me, that required a change in venue to support the change in mind-set. Stanford, California, is not an awful change in venue.

I had already put Karen through a lot in our relationship during my entrepreneurial streak. I had a great job at IBM in my late twenties, but I really wanted to have my own company. The start-up of Berbee Information Networks Corporation was stressful for both of us. Karen was used to that. Even so, medical school was a bit more extreme because I asked her to leave all of our friends and family in Madison and to move to California, where we didn't know anybody.

I viewed it as being on a job assignment for four years. I was busy every day and studying every night. It wasn't the same for Karen. She didn't know anybody, and that was hard for her. Eventually, she found that Stanford has wonderful adult-education classes and was accepted to a writing-certificate program.

RESIDENCY REALITIES

When I neared graduation, it was time to apply to residency programs. Residency is the period after medical school when you receive training specific to your chosen specialty—emergency medicine, in my case. The duration can vary from three years to more than ten years, depending on your specialty. Usually, graduating medical students apply to about twenty different programs, hoping to get into one that's in their preferred location. I only wanted to be part of a program that would take us back to Madison, and there was only one: the University of Wisconsin Hospital and Clinics (UW). I did a fair amount of networking with physicians and staff at the UW, hoping that would pay off in getting me into the emergency-medicine residency program. I wasn't sure that would work out. Medical school makes you humble; I couldn't be sure they would accept me. One of the individuals I made sure to meet with was Dr. Azita Hamedani, the chair of the Department of Emergency Medicine. After I was accepted into the Wisconsin residency program, she became my mentor.

Medical school wasn't easy, but it wasn't particularly hard, either. I wasn't first in my class, but I wasn't last. Residency, however, was extraordinarily difficult. It was by far the hardest thing I've ever done because of the hours and the emotional stress. You work overnight, then a few nights, and then during the day. You're in the hospital virtually every day. When you're not in the hospital, you're home sleeping. When you're not sleeping, you're spending hours doing the required documentation on the patients you saw on your shift the night before. Any free time you have is spent studying in preparation for the board exams.

While working in the ED, you see so many of society's problems on every shift that you can't help but absorb some of the ugliness. You never get the chance to recover emotionally or physically because you're always working and always tired. I had some really bad times during residency when it was, sometimes, difficult to see the reason for going on and completing it.

For example, one night on a very busy shift, I went in to see a patient with psychiatric problems. He did not speak English or any language for which we had translators. His family had done a "dump and run." He was obviously very troubled and needed help, but there was no way to get any history. I was tired, mentally overloaded, and empathetically drained. I was unprofessional, and worse, unkind. I'm ashamed of the way I treated that man.

Everybody warned me about how hard it would be. I would say, "Nah, that's not going to happen to me. I'm older. I know myself." That was another gift of this experience: the knowledge that I don't know myself as well as I thought I did. I remind myself every day to doubt my own infallibility.

I was lucky to have Dr. Hamedani, the emergency-medicine department chair, as my mentor. She is not only one of the best physicians I know but also a talented leader with keen insight into human nature. She taught me two important lessons about emergency medicine.

First, most of what we see is routine, obvious, and nonlife-threatening. What we must not miss are the nonobvious, life-threatening conditions that may appear to be routine. If you diagnose a fever in a two-year-old as a viral illness, you will be correct 99.9 percent of the time. It's the exceptional emergency physician that does not miss meningitis in that other 0.1 percent. This requires a high level of vigilance and constant doubting of your own infallibility.

Second, although we do very dramatic things on rare occasions, it is the routine comfort and reassurance that we provide to every patient that defines our profession. It's the ability to comfort the fifteenth patient who shows up with a cough.

I'm often asked, "Would you do it again?" No way! But if you ask the question differently, "Are you glad you did it?" Absolutely! Is that any different than many other challenging yet rewarding experiences? Thank goodness we go into some efforts naïve, or we would never attempt them at all

Emergency Medicine: A Natural Choice

I chose my specialty because I love procedures, and I get to do a lot of them in emergency medicine, from mundane procedures such as laceration repairs to dramatic procedures such as intubations, chest tubes, and central lines. One day, in the ED, a patient with a collapsed lung had blood in his chest. He needed a chest tube to drain the blood and reinflate the lung. It's a life-saving emergency

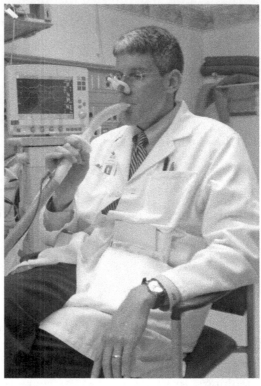

Jim experiences positive-pressure ventilation. This is a device used to help critically ill patients breathe.

procedure. I vividly remember cutting into his chest and feeling his lung with my finger as I advanced the chest tube. As I was doing this, all I could think was, *Wow, seven years ago I was the chairman of an information-technology company!*

Some of my favorite stories involve our older citizens. I had just put a ninety-two-year-old woman's dislocated shoulder back in place, and I apologized to her for "manhandling her." She looked me straight in the eye and said, "Oh my, it's been quite some time since I've been manhandled." I still blush thinking of this wonderful patient who "made" my entire shift. Another time I was performing a neurologic exam on an eighty-nine-year-old woman. I asked her to push me away with her hand. She said to me, "I never push a man away!" I laugh just telling that story. Then there was the time I treated a sick but stable eighty-five-year-old man with terminal cancer. He asked me where I was from. When I told him I was from Madison, which is known for being very liberal, he asked me if I was a Democrat (he, clearly, was a proud Republican). I told him that I was the only doctor in the hospital, and then I asked him if he really cared. That got a huge laugh from the patient, his wife, and his daughter. Those are just a few examples of the wonderful human interactions I experience during every shift. Such interactions are truly a gift that is not to be dismissed or diminished, and they show that we have so much more in common than the trivial issues that separate us.

> **Thank goodness we go into some efforts naïve, or we would never attempt them at all.**

At this stage in my life, I have no interest in working standard hours. I want to be absolutely in charge of when, where, and how much I work. With emergency medicine, I can do that. It's shift work in a hospital emergency center, and I can work as many or as few shifts as I want. I get daily calls and e-mails from recruiters who need emergency physicians all over the country. The demand for my specialty is bottomless. In my case, I choose to work where I can give back to the people of Wisconsin. This is the state that nurtured me, first at the university and then at my business. I work the shifts that fit in well with my other activities. And I see—just as I had hoped—a lot of medicine.

I've already had one career. I'm not trying to climb the ladder or establish a traditional career in medicine. I'm doing this because I want to be involved. I want to make a difference. I want to get my hands dirty. I want to keep grounded. That's something medicine really does well. It's easy to lose perspective after you've sold a company. I didn't want to turn into that guy who loses touch with the way people live and the reality of the world. Seeing people's day-to-day struggles and issues prevents you from becoming too much of a jerk. It also makes you very grateful for all that you have been given.

Although I choose to practice emergency medicine in deep gratitude for my life, my patients give me the gift of humanity with each shift.

WORTH THE RISK

The risk in going to medical school at my age wasn't financial; it was reputational. I didn't want to fail. I told everybody what I was doing and they expected a lot from me. I was worried that I would get there and either completely flame out because I couldn't do the work or, worse, realize that I hated what I was doing.

Medicine was the only second career I've considered, and it took a long time to see the rewards of that pursuit. It has been ten years since I started down this road. I'm now fifty-two years old. I've passed my written and oral board exams, and I'm fully board-certified as an emergency physician. I'm working the right number of hours. I look forward to every shift, and I really enjoy the work. I get a lot of satisfaction out of it, but when I'm done with my shift, I'm done.

I've been working for the past two years on a better medical device, the otoscope, that is primarily used to examine children's ears. Although it's a seemingly simple device, it's quite a challenge to create one that gives a superior view of the ear drum while integrating with

Jim (on the right) working on shift after completing residency. His brother, Peter Berbee (sitting to the left), also works in the emergency center.

clinical applications and being robust enough to use in the clinical environment. I don't know if it will ever reach the market, but I'm enjoying the effort. I am fortunate to have both Dr. Azita Hamedani and Dr. Greg Rebella as my partners in this endeavor.

I invest in multiple companies, some with a medical focus. One of the most rewarding and successful is a Madison-based cancer-treatment technology company started by a University of Wisconsin radiologist.

I've never been more contented in my life.

STILL TIME FOR CHARITY AND COMMITTEES

Karen and I recently made a $10 million gift to the Department of Emergency Medicine at the University of Wisconsin Hospital and Clinics to double the size of the emergency area and create a large number of endowed professorships for the department. The facility will improve care for citizens in our community, and the research positions will improve emergency-medicine care globally. This is the perfect fit for our health-care-focused foundation. We know that our investment is going to be used wisely under the oversight of my mentor, Dr. Hamedani. It's rare to be able to deploy charitable dollars with absolute confidence in the desired outcome.

In 2004, the CEO of my former company, Paul Shain, and I started the Berbee Derby, a Thanksgiving Day race in Madison. All of the proceeds go toward the Technology Education Foundation, which provides private funding for technology in classrooms and nonprofit organizations. Today the race attracts more than six thousand runners who come to exercise and celebrate before what, for many, will be a big holiday dinner. The race has raised over a million dollars for the community since its inception.

I'm proud to be on the board of trustees of the Wisconsin Alumni Research Foundation (WARF). The foundation has a portfolio of more than $2.5 billion, with thousands of patents from inventors at the University of Wisconsin Madison. My otoscope work is covered by two WARF patents. The state of Wisconsin, as do most states, faces budget challenges. I like being able to help an institution that has done so much for me and my family, not to mention the world. The WARF board is made up of Wisconsin alumni who have been highly successful in one way or another. I was fortunate enough to be asked to join the WARF board because of my business background, and I joined in my first year of residency. When I was in residency, I used to do some major maneuvering to be able to attend the board meetings. The meetings take place over two or three days, three or four times a year. That would be all the days off I'd have in the month, so I'd have to trade days and work twenty-seven days in a row to get the time off. Now that I'm done with training, I have the flexibility to be involved in all the conference calls and committee meetings. I can participate at a much higher level than I was able to before, which is great.

Life in the Emergency Department

My engineering background and my experience with Berbee Information Networks makes me overly sensitive to computer problems at the hospital, which happen frequently. When I have my hands full with sick people and the radiology program goes down and locks up the whole computer system, I run out of patience quickly. At the same time, my business experience lets me take the wider view, which is that hospitals are complex systems. We spend huge amounts of time documenting things, more for insurance, billing, and legal purposes than for their medical value. From the patients' perspective, I appear to come in and spend five minutes with them, and they never see me again. From my perspective, I spend half an hour doing the paperwork associated with the visit.

My business background has been useful in the emergency center. I have a very short amount of time to build rapport with a patient and to get to the bottom of what's going on, including asking probing questions about private and personal things. The sales and marketing skills I learned in business are helpful in getting to know people and build trust with them quickly. I have to present myself to the patient as someone capable and trustworthy. The people skills I developed while running my business have helped make me sensitive about what's needed at a particular time with patients. Is now the time to joke or not joke? Does the elderly patient want the children involved in the discussion? Do I need to be concerned about child abuse with this pediatric patient? Does this patient have the social support to be safe at home?

Escape versus Embrace

My message to someone thinking of a big career switch is don't be afraid. Think it through and understand the upside and downside of the decision. Be clear about how you view what the world is going to be like after the dust has settled and you've made the switch. Most importantly, be clear about why you're doing it. Is it because it's something you really want to do? Or are you looking for an escape from something you hate? Do it because you're going toward something.

I'd like to leave you with a paraphrase of a quote that has meant a lot to me. The source of my paraphrase is Gary Comer, the founder of Lands' End. Gary was an investor in Berbee but passed away shortly before the company was sold. I wish I had been able to thank him personally for believing in me. Here, in essence, is what he said: "Because I was able to do it, I know that it can still be done in America today, and I wish you the 'little bit of luck' you'll need."

Jim's story may be the most "180" of all of the great stories in this book. I really like the lines near the end of his story about going toward something and not running away from something. That is an incredibly important lesson for folks considering doing something new with their careers—and their lives.

Jim is driven by a desire to help people and a passion for learning, according to friend Paul Shain. His enthusiasm and humility have been key to his success in business, medicine, and beyond.

"Jim is a man of high integrity and complete honesty with a very direct communication style, whether the news is good or bad," Shain said. "There are no surprises with Jim, and he is always open to continuous learning and hearing others' thoughts and ideas."

Jim took a huge leap to learn many new skills and enter a completely new world. I'm not sure how many people become doctors in their forties, but if Jim can do that, the rest of us can likely take on just about any career 180 switch we can imagine.

Thanks again to Dr. Jim for his great achievements— and for his inspiration.

SUE ELA

Growing the Legacy of the Orchards

"The apple doesn't fall far from the tree."

PROVERB

Over the course of forty years in the Wisconsin health-care system, Sue Ela rose through the ranks to become the most senior female health-care executive in the state. Sue served as COO for the multibillion-dollar company Aurora Health Care, managing tens of thousands of full-time employees, more than 1,500 physicians, fifteen medical centers, eighty retail pharmacies, home care, hospice, social services, and more.

Although she excelled at the intense responsibilities of the role, Sue stepped out of the health-care ranks to take on the COO position of a company even closer to her heart: her family's new hard-cider company.

This is Sue's career 180 story.

===

A few years ago, I knew nothing about the cider-making process. I didn't have a reason to. I was part of a team running a multibillion-dollar, health-care system and was responsible for the jobs of more than thirty thousand full-time employees. Cider brewing wasn't exactly part of the job description.

Once I stepped down from my health-care role after forty years in that industry, I had the remarkable opportunity to work with some of the people I love most in the world—my husband and three children—in a trade I never thought I'd be involved in: cider making.

Over little more than a year, I went from knowing nothing about apple fermentation to creating an award-winning cider from scratch with my family. Ela Cider Company is recognized as much for its attention to sustainability and social responsibility as it is for the taste of its Stone Silo cider, the product of more than one hundred years of Ela family history, made from apples grown in a community where the Elas have lived since the mid-1800s.

Our family's cider company is more than just a surprisingly successful enterprise; it's the culmination of my skills, my passion for people, my work ethic, and my incredible love for my family. I never imagined myself in this role, but today I can't imagine doing anything else.

A MOTHER'S INSPIRATION

My first nursing job was as an RN at the Milwaukee Children's Hospital, now the Children's Hospital of Wisconsin. I was determined to be like my mother, who was one of the first nurses in her day to have a bachelor's degree beyond her nursing diploma. She was a night supervisor and very proud of her profession. When I was a little girl, she would come home and tell me about the people she had helped that night in the emergency room or about those who had lost a family member and how she was able to support them.

It wasn't just a job, she told me; it was a privilege. I wanted to be just like her. I told everyone I wanted to be a nurse when I grew up, and that's exactly what I did.

I went to a two-year nursing program straight out of high school and then, after receiving a scholarship from the hospital where my mother worked, I earned my associate's degree in nursing. Right after I earned that degree, I attended Marquette University and received my bachelor's degree in nursing.

It wasn't required—you can be a nurse with a two- or three-year degree—but it was really important to me that I earn it as my mom had done so many years before. I also knew that if I wanted to hold leadership positions in health care, I would need an advanced degree.

NATURAL-BORN LEADER

I worked at the Children's Hospital of Wisconsin for about twenty years. During that time, I not only earned my master's degree but also held pretty much every job a nurse could have, from graduate-level nurse to vice president of patient-care services.

And I'll tell you, I don't think I applied for a single one of those roles. They were offered to me because I wasn't afraid to speak up. I have always been an assertive, natural leader, which may have been influenced by the fact that I was the sixth of seven children. Being from a large family helped me develop a strong sense of independence and self-sufficiency—and when you have three older brothers, the incessant teasing gives you a thick skin pretty fast.

In each of my positions at Children's Hospital, I learned the value of leadership, patient advocacy, collaboration, and teamwork. It was also in those roles that I found my voice: how to say things in a way that did not threaten or antagonize colleagues, thereby maintaining our relationship.

It was a period of significant transition in nursing. When I first started, nurses still wore caps and were expected to stand when a physician entered the unit. I refused to do either. After all, caps got in the way of traction, and why should I stand if I was charting and it was my first chance to sit down all day?

Early on, some of my superiors recognized (and tolerated) my leadership abilities. It was a period of intense unionization, and instead of unionizing, I chose to work for change from within. I did stage a sit-in at the director's office, the hospital met our demands, and I was rewarded with a promotion to manager. As such, I became one of those really lucky people who were able to advance their career while still staying in the same community where they raised their kids.

A New Opportunity

In 1995, one of the biggest companies in Milwaukee, Aurora Health Care, recruited me to be the president of the Aurora Visiting Nurse Association, Home Care Division. I was attracted to Aurora because of its mission: "There is a better way to provide health care." The CEO at the time, Ed Howe, had a reputation as a visionary, and I saw my interview as a great opportunity to meet him. Twenty minutes in, I was hired. It was one of the best decisions I ever made. For the next fifteen years, Ed was my mentor, advisor, champion, and friend.

After I took the position as president of the Visiting Nurse Association, Home Care Division, Aurora promoted me to the newly created role of chief clinical officer. I led the care-management/quality function in partnership with the chief medical officer. Aurora then added a regional president role for me and then another. After ten years of increasing my responsibilities, Ed retired as CEO. Chief operating officer Nick Turkal was appointed to succeed him, and I took Nick's COO position.

It was truly an amazing career path for me. In forty years, I went from being a graduate nurse to the COO of an integrated health-care system that earned about $4.2 billion in annual revenue. Aurora Health Care had thirty thousand full-time employees, 1,500 physicians serving patients in 290 locations in ninety communities, fifteen medical centers, and eighty retail pharmacies, and home care, hospice, and social services. I was responsible for the quality and service outcomes of all those hospitals, physicians, and clinical services.

DOING IT ALL IN HEALTH CARE

I believe my collaboration and value-driven leadership skills helped to fuel my quick progression at Aurora while the organization worked to become an integrated health-care system. I also owe much of my success to Ed, my mentor, who opened many doors and often saw things in me that I didn't see in myself. I was often outside my comfort zone, but I always knew I could count on his unwavering support, even when I made mistakes, of which there were plenty.

I didn't become COO of Aurora immediately, of course. It happened through a series of progressively responsible positions, a little more on my plate each time. I helped design and implement two or three hospitals during my tenure and coordinated gathering the approvals and raising money philanthropically for a residential hospice at Aurora, the first in the state for both adults and children. I testified before Congress and did just about everything I thought I could possibly do in health care.

At the same time, I was very involved in community leadership. My first love was always children and children's health, so I took leadership positions with a number of community nonprofits in Milwaukee, including cochairing the United Way campaign and serving on and chairing the boards of the Boys and Girls Clubs and Big Brothers Big Sisters. I still sit on a number of community boards and participate in community fundraising efforts.

TIME FOR A CLEAN SLATE

But I was starting to get restless. I was in my late fifties at this point, and as the COO of Aurora, I was in a hugely responsible position.

I loved the job, and I loved working with a physician partner who was also my clinical leadership partner as well as Aurora's CEO. I gradually realized that it was time to look in another direction, however. It took me almost a year to make the decision, but in the end, I knew that if I were ever going to try something else, this would be the time to do it.

My husband was my confidant and advisor. He encouraged me to take some time off, smell the roses, and then decide what I wanted. He is my biggest fan to this day.

While the CEO was supportive, he was naturally surprised and didn't want me to leave. In fact, he did everything he could to encourage me to stay, including offering to redesign my job to see if it would suit my needs better, which was nice. But I think that was also part of it. A slightly different version of my current job wasn't what I was looking for. I just needed a complete break, not a different job in the same field but more of a clean slate. I needed a sabbatical from work to figure out what I wanted to do next, to find out what made sense to me.

I didn't leave my job quickly. It was very important for me to accomplish the transition from my responsibilities smoothly and be sure my family was financially secure before I made any kind of move. I didn't want to chance putting my family or retirement at risk. But at the same time, life is short. I have always heard that you don't regret the things you do as much as you regret the things you don't do. I didn't want to wonder if I could have done something different.

Sue, her son, John, and her husband, Tom, with the fruits of their labor.

I value my family life immensely, and I wanted more time to be with my husband and kids as they lived their adult lives. We seemed to have the ideal balance as they were growing up. I had a need for impact and influence that was probably best exercised outside the home. My husband had a design and construction business that allowed him flexibility and a home office, and he had the patience and sense of curiosity and fun that help growing children thrive. As time went on, though, I felt satisfied with my accomplishments and contributions on a larger scale, and I wanted to put family first in a new endeavor. So I took the risk and followed my values.

The Good in the Bad

For the first year after I left Aurora, I didn't want to do much of anything. I just wanted to relax, see how tired I really was, and do what I needed to do to take care of myself and my health.

My open schedule became a blessing in many ways because, during that year, some of my family members and close friends had health issues that I wouldn't have been able to devote nearly as much time to if I had been working.

First, my sister-in-law was struck by lightning. It was bizarre and it affected her enormously. She had an intensive two-year recovery, and during that time, I was able to visit her in Madison once a week and help her recover.

Around that time, one of my cousins was diagnosed with lung cancer. Fortunately, I was able to be there for him and help him navigate the health-care system. I also supported my elderly parents during that time, helping them manage their health-care needs and relocating them to Milwaukee to be closer to us.

Then my closest friend in the world was diagnosed with ALS, all within that first year away from Aurora. It was a difficult time, but I just kept thinking, *This is fortuitous. What a privilege to be able to help people understand such a complicated health-care system.* I was also very grateful for the opportunity to help the people I love when they needed me. I could never, ever have done that if I had been working.

Exploring New Options

Taking care of so many people who are dear to me was truly a privilege, and I felt great about it. But after about a year and a half, I began to get a little itchy. I wanted to do something else, but I wasn't sure what.

A physician friend of mine called to tell me about a software company he was starting for orthopedic outcomes. I'd worked with him at Aurora and knew him to be a really good person who always had innovative ideas, so when he asked if I wanted to help him start his company, I thought, Sure, *why not?* It sounded like fun and a way to stretch myself.

I worked with him for about eighteen months, helping him get the company off the ground, hiring developers, and setting up all the systems. My perspective as a customer, rather than as a provider, was particularly beneficial as he navigated the health-care system. It was really fun, but it wasn't something I wanted to turn into a second career.

Sue with her family. Front row: Sue, Tom. Back row: John, Annie, Julia, and Julia's husband, Phillip Sasser.

BE CIDER SELF

Then my son started talking to me about what he was doing at our cousins' orchard in Rochester, Wisconsin.

He'd been interning there for a while, helping them make a nonalcoholic cider that had a kind of cult following in southeastern Wisconsin. But they didn't have a hard cider. I had read an article in *The Wall Street Journal* about the rising popularity of hard cider as a gluten-free, fruit-based beverage. Major beverage companies were getting into the business, and local ciders were following in the footsteps of the craft-beer movement as more people became interested in eating and drinking local.

"What if you made a hard cider from Ela Orchard apples?" I asked him.

He already did his own home brewing, so he took me up on it. He and my husband began fermenting and experimenting, and after about fifty different batches, he hit on one that was great.

So we started a business: Ela Cider Company. Since the orchard's ownership was already rather complicated, the owners supported our decision to form a separate company that leveraged the strength of our shared family name. I had some confidence after the successful software start-up, and I knew that leadership and business skills were universal. It was also a low-risk venture financially. Our biggest concern was navigating the family dynamics successfully, and we were all committed to doing so.

It's truly a family business too. My husband, Tom, manages facilities and production; my son, John, helps Tom with production and does the fermenting; my daughter, Julia, handles the marketing; and my daughter, Annie, does the photography. I run operations, sales, and finance. We set the mission, vision, goals, strategy, and plan together—all of those things that I did as an executive.

And it's funny because, in a way, it's even more challenging than being the COO of a multibillion-dollar company. Whereas, before, I had staff and assistants and resources, now it's just my family and me. Not only am I having to learn new skills that I used to have staff for, but I'm also having to find a way for us to have family time that's separate from the cider business. That was the biggest adjustment, actually: making sure we had off-business time when we weren't talking about cider or making to-do lists. It's a challenge, but at the same time, it's a lot of fun to take our natural abilities and turn them into a little business.

After forty years in the health-care industry, I'm certainly surprised to find myself running a cider company with my family. But I'm also grateful because I feel very lucky. I'm lucky to be able to do this and lucky to be able to work with my family and our cousins at Ela Orchard and with those in the farm-to-table movement, supporting family farms and young entrepreneurs in their dream.

THE FAMILY CONNECTION

The roots in Rochester, Wisconsin, run deep in my husband's family. Rochester is a little town at a little crossroads where his great-grandfather, Richard Emerson Ela, settled in the 1800s and started a business building farm implements. His business did so well, in fact, that he built a factory across the river and expanded with a farmhouse that still stands today.

There's an Ela Park, an Ela Road, and, of course, an Ela Orchard, which has been in operation since the 1920s. It is owned by our cousins Bob Willard and Edwin Ela. They're the ones who grow and harvest the apples that we buy and press before putting the juice through the cider-making process. Our cousin Bob's wife, Jane Hamilton, is the best-selling author of *Book of Ruth* and, in April 2016, released her latest book, *The Excellent Lombards*, which features the orchard prominently.

Sue and her cousin Bob Willard stroll through the Ela apple orchard.

Our son, John, graduated from Yale College in 2011 with a degree in environmental history. He had experience in environmental education, sustainability practices, and home brewing. He was always drawn to the orchard and approached the owners to ask if he could serve as an apprentice there. He was drawn by the land, the people, and the family history. That connection planted the seed for our cider business.

The apples in the orchard range from Jonagold to McIntosh. We use a careful balance of varietals to make our inaugural hard cider, Stone Silo, which is named for a one-hundred-year-old silo on the property. This year, we are releasing Barn Cat, a drier, tarter cider, designed to appeal to evolving tastes.

Award-Winning Cider

Ela Cider Company is a wonderful family business. It's a lot of work, but it's also really, really fun. And it's paid off! After only one year of production, Stone Silo was selected out of 160 ciders

submitted from across the United States for the national 2016 Good Food Award. The Good Food Award goes not only to the best-tasting product but also to the one that meets the award's rigorous sustainability and social-responsibility criteria. This year, Stone Silo also received the silver medal from the Great Lakes International Cider and Perry Competition in the New World category.

Ela Cider Company's Stone Silo is already winning awards, including the national 2016 Good Food Award.

The cider meets our own rigorous criteria, as well. We wanted to make a product that was high quality and reflected the excellence of the orchard and the people who live in it and around it. It's not just about making hard cider; it's about tradition, respect, and creating a family legacy. Sustainability is important to us, but it was easy to achieve. It's a core tenet of the orchard's operations, which gave us a road map to follow for our own business.

Do I miss working in the health-care industry? No, not really. I'm still friends with the people I worked with at Children's and at

Aurora, and I'm still able to use my nursing and administrative skills, which I do all the time. Today I'm doing what I love and what I'm good at, and I get to do it with my family. And it certainly helps that it involves delicious food and apples.

My career 180 meant starting fresh at a time when I was wiser than ever. I learned that I could reapply my experience and wisdom to a new endeavor in life and achieve success despite the risk. While a major career pivot can be intimidating and take time for you to discover, it can also be greater than you ever imagined.

> **Today I'm doing what I love and what I'm good at, and I get to do it with my family.**

If I were to offer any piece of advice to someone considering a career 180, as I did, I would say this: Don't let yourself wonder if you could have done something differently. Weigh the decision carefully and talk to those it will affect directly, but if it's doable, absolutely take the risk and follow your heart. Life is short. Don't let yourself look back one day and wonder what could have been. Just let go and do it.

Sue is a great lady. I had the pleasure of visiting the Ela Orchard in Rochester, Wisconsin. I walked the land with Sue and her cousin Bob Willard, who runs the operation. It is a peaceful place where you can feel the commitment to quality and doing things right. I even got to see the stone silo that is the namesake of the Ela Cider Company's flagship product.

When I spoke about Sue with her former boss Nick Turkal, the CEO of Aurora Health Care, he said, "Sue cares about people so much, and she is always committed to achieving goals. If she wants to build a great cider company, then consider it done." I certainly saw and felt that as we toured the beautiful property.

Another longtime professional friend of Sue, Barbara Bowman, said, "Sue is focused on quality and relationships—and those things are important in any business endeavor, including the cider business."

I like this story because Sue did not leave Aurora for a new career right away. She took some time off and provided care to folks in need, but now she has jumped with gusto and passion into the hard-cider business and has already won awards. I have absolutely no doubt this new business will succeed. In fact, I just bought a case of Stone Silo cider right before it sold out for the entire season. I can tell you it is absolutely great!

ROBERT FINKEL

Brewing His Way to Happiness

"Beer is proof that God loves us and wants us to be happy."

BENJAMIN FRANKLIN

Glass jars full of juniper berries, chili peppers, and black walnuts line the distressed wood shelves at Forbidden Root, Chicago's first botanic brewery. Past the curtained private dining area, gleaming silver tanks hold beers infused with plant essences from Forbidden Root's custom "flavor torpedo." Upstairs, hundreds of herbs, flowers, and other plants in gold packets fill the dark, wooden drawers of a massive card catalog. This is the vision of Robert Finkel and a far cry from the venture-capital career he left behind.

Robert, the founder of the private-investment firm Prism Capital, spent twenty-five years supporting other entrepreneurs before transitioning into a world of tinctures, elixirs, and international bittering units (IBUs). As Forbidden Root's self-dubbed rootmaster, Robert has combined his business acumen and passion for natural ingredients to take people on a journey through beer.

Robert is a smart, interesting, and colorful character, as I am sure you will agree when you read his career 180 story.

―――――――――――――――――――――――――――――――――――――

I started my first company, a jewelry business, when I was ten years old. I invested the profits, which brought me to Wall Street. After business school, my interest in growing companies led me to a successful career in venture capital, where I eventually headed an investment firm with $190 million in assets under management.

While I loved identifying new opportunities to add value to businesses, what became the private-equity industry slowly lost its allure for me. It became more mercenary and less about helping people develop the companies into which they had poured their blood, sweat, and tears. I wanted to work where I could be my aspirational self, rooted in a community of like-minded people. A few years ago, I found it.

As the founder of Forbidden Root, Chicago's first botanic brewery, I get to revel in my eccentric side, creatively develop unique products from natural ingredients, and build a business that will live on. When I began pursuing this dream a few years ago, my oldest friend said it best: "Few know that you just took a twenty-five-year break between business school and your true passion."

Robert greets Alderman Joe Moreno during Forbidden Root's opening night.

LITTLE BUSINESSMAN, BIG DREAMS

I grew up in Manhattan, the youngest of my parents' six children. As the runt of the litter, I was hungry to prove myself. At seven years old, I carried around a beat-up, leather briefcase stuffed with my father's old annual reports.

It wasn't long until I had occasion to use that suitcase. While I was at a shell store on vacation with my family in Palm Beach, my mother gave me $5 to buy souvenirs, which I invested in small colorful shells along with holes, jump rings, and chains. I assembled these parts into necklaces and sold them to the store down the strip from our hotel. The owner paid me $2.50 per necklace, and I had spent less than a dollar each to make them. I had my first taste of entrepreneurial success.

The store owner asked me for one more round of necklaces before I left for home, and I expanded the business to the hotel staff while still on vacation. When back in school, I would spend a couple of hours in the lobby of our apartment building, selling to neighbors as they walked in. At eleven years old, I announced to my parents that I wouldn't be going to sleep-away camp that year. A hot summer walking the streets of New York to develop my burgeoning jewelry business sounded great to me. I visited the Garment District, found the right suppliers, and began sourcing my shell jewelry wholesale.

Through my growing connections, I met a sales rep, although I didn't know what a sales rep was at the time. She took me under her wing and agreed to represent my jewelry line to national chains, including Bloomingdale's, Neiman Marcus, Bullock's, and May Company. I called my business RAF Creations and learned how to build a cohesive jewelry business, including how to handle accounting and operations. None of my customers knew that I was barely a teenager or that my mother had to fill out my invoices because I still had the handwriting of a child.

OPENING THE BLACK BOX

I wound down RAF Creations at the ripe old age of fourteen, investing my profits in art and the stock market. My experience had piqued my interest in business and finance, and I knew I wanted to pursue a career on Wall Street.

At sixteen, I secured my own summer job at PaineWebber. It was the first of five wonderful summers with the company. I joined the firm after college in one of those high-minded, rotational programs in which you get the chance to see the financial industry from many angles. I ended up in the company's mergers and acquisitions group.

I earned my bachelor's degree from Johns Hopkins University and my MBA from Harvard Business School, where I formed and sold an optical cleaning-cloth business in my second year. While weighing my career options, I became intrigued by the venture-capital world. The prospect of investing in growing companies was compelling. I was on the road less traveled, as people didn't yet refer to raising venture capital as an industry. Today, Chicago has about 120 venture-capital firms; in 1989 it had eight. To me, the fast-paced, mysterious world of venture capital was irresistible. I was determined to get into that black box and see what was inside.

Building a Career, Deal by Deal

I spent four years at Wind Point Partners, learning from smart, focused professionals how to (1) identify, evaluate, negotiate, and invest in good companies; (2) add value; and (3) exit. After Wind Point, I became what's known as a sponsorless private-equity professional, a deal-by-deal guy. It's a relentlessly tough job. You find a great company, negotiate the purchase, and then tell the company, "I'll be right back," so you can go source the funding and close.

I founded Prism Capital in 1998. It was one of Illinois State's first equity-oriented, small-business investment companies. My partners and I then raised a debt fund to complement and support the equity fund (Prism Capital) and further invested in a total of forty companies supported by these two funds. As the managing partner of $190 million in assets under management, I was on my way.

Looking for a New Adventure

I got into the venture-capital business in search of an adventure. I'm an energetic person, and I wanted a career in which I could pour that positive energy into something equally positive. Backing thoughtful, passionate entrepreneurs with a unique vision of how to approach their markets was a lot of fun in the early years, but the venture-capital industry started to change and became more about effective asset management.

The depressing fact remains that the year in which a fund is raised usually has a greater impact on outcome and returns than individual investing skills. Our equity fund was one of the country's top-performing, small-business investment company (SBIC) equity funds for funds started in 1999, yet the timing of the investment period affected the ability to generate good returns. It's a tough, very long-term business, in which there aren't a lot of opportunities to be creative, and control over life and outcomes is less than optimal.

The recession that hit in 2008 forced my partners and me to think hard about what we wanted to do. We could have raised another fund, but we couldn't raise a bigger fund and still be able to achieve the returns we wanted. I had to decide whether to wait things out or pivot to something new.

Forbidden Root has a rare "floating" draft tower that allows for less obtrusive views and encourages conversation.

THE POWER OF A PIVOT

At a certain point, I chose to pivot. I wrote a book titled *The Masters of Private Equity and Venture Capital*, published by McGraw-Hill Business Books. I didn't know it at the time, but I was writing my thank-you letter to the best-of-breed investors, whom I wanted to showcase as models of success. They were craftsmen, and they got into the business for reasons other than simply making as much money as they could.

As a consumer, I was always researching things, be they places to travel or dietary supplements. My interest in supplements and nutrition comes partly from my family. My aunt started sending me vitamins when I was seven years old. I quickly discovered that many supplement manufacturers were citing decades-old studies as evidence to support their nutritional claims. There was no real research to prove that multivitamins, a $7 billion business in the United States, had credible evidence of benefits. That was a revelation to me: people spend billions, annually, on vitamins, but many are more like an insurance policy than an evidence-based treatment.

I am drawn to unaddressed opportunities that have lasting impact, be they profit or nonprofit. I decided to establish a supplement research center, the Center for Nutritional Literacy, which could provide consumers with the information they needed to make educated decisions about what goes into their bodies. I knew that it needed to be a nonprofit to avoid any perception of bias. The time I was spending at Prism had lessened substantially, allowing me to focus on this new venture.

I invested in developing a unique online resource and assembled a world-class scientific advisory board to create a proprietary set of algorithms that would provide evidence-based research on supplements. I made a lot of progress over a year and a half, and as I was on the brink of final market testing, my interests took me in another direction instead.

For the Love of Root Beer

I am a sort of foodie by birth. My grandfather invented and fabricated the Thermolater, the coffee dispenser used by Chock Full O'Nuts at its retail locations. In the 1950s, my dad ran marketing for Welch's and then spent time in the liquor industry. My brother-in-law chaired the Fancy Food Show, a huge trade expo, and is a veteran of the specialty-food business. I love flavor, I love pairing, and I love introducing someone to an unusual culinary experience.

As I immersed myself in studying plant-based supplements, my interest in botanics began to flourish. One of the great botanical-based drinks is root beer. The original beverage was alcoholic and brewed with plants and spices, including sassafras (now deemed carcinogenic), wintergreen, ginger, vanilla, and birch. I wondered why there wasn't a commercially available alcoholic root beer, and the seedling of the idea for Forbidden Root took hold.

I knew I couldn't pursue this idea and also launch the Center for Nutritional Literacy. Ultimately, the call of the beer was too strong. I wanted to get back to the basics of developing, making, marketing, and selling a product, just as I had done years before in the jewelry business. I still believe in the Center, and I hope to bring it to fruition at some point with someone else leading the charge.

More Than a One-Trick Pony

While I was passionate about the idea of brewing an authentic root beer, I didn't have a background in beer, although, courtesy of Prism,

I did have an exposure to craft beer. In the early 2000s, one of my partners at Prism came up with the idea of doing craft-beer tastings for the venture and private-equity community, so we coined it Novemberfest. For six years, we poured a variety of delicious beers, and I was struck by the wide continuum of styles and tastes. The notion of an alcoholic root beer rattled in my head, and when I recognized what I believed to be a clear gap in a consumer offering, I had to investigate.

I found that one of the world's most recognized craft-beer authorities, Randy Mosher, lived in Chicago, and I reached out to him to solicit his honest opinion. If I couldn't get a third party to validate my hypothesis that an alcoholic root beer was a great opportunity, I didn't want to spin my wheels.

We met for lunch at a favorite Japanese restaurant, where he walked up in his earnest, casual way, wearing an Indiana Jones-like hat. When I told him of my plans, he was concerned that root beer was a one-trick pony. I agreed, and he urged me to think more holistically. Together, we developed the idea of a botanical-based brewery: designing beers around a flavor profile, rather than brewing to a particular style.

Forbidden Root designed and uses a custom "flavor torpedo" to inject its beers with botanical essences, infusing its hallmark unique flavors.

While it may seem intuitive, it's a novel idea in the brewing world. Just as a dog breeder focuses on the perfect American Kennel Club-approved characteristics of a cocker spaniel, brewers focus on time and temperature to create the perfect *hefeweizen*. With all due respect to the craftsmen who make beautiful beer, we do not adhere to guidelines for style.

Instead, we develop unique flavors and profiles and design the beer around the flavors. Our ideas come from my travel, Randy's encyclopedic palate, and our head brewer, BJ Pichman, as well as collaboration and experimentation. The natural ingredients that flavor our beer come from all over the globe. The only rule is that whatever we produce has to feature ingredients or combinations not previously experienced. For instance, we're developing a line of beers called Hive Minded, which will feature one of more than one hundred varieties of monofloral honeys in my reference collection.

When people drink our beers, we want them to be transported to a different time and place. To do that, we search exhaustively for just the right flavors. For our Sublime Ginger beer, we sampled forty ginger varieties before choosing the right one. The lemon myrtle that we import from Australia imparts the cleanest lemon-drop flavor we could find. Honeybush from South Africa gives the flavor a round, tropical note. When you drink Sublime Ginger, we want you to feel as if you were walking on the beaches of Key West on a clear, sunny day, with the gentle vibration of waves crashing in the background.

A Different View of Risk

Most people would probably call opening a brewery without any prior brewing knowledge a high-risk decision. I believed I could mitigate a portion of that risk. My venture-capital experience taught me how to manage risk, plan for the long term, develop a brand strategy, foster a culture of participation, and focus on value instead of cash flow, in the early years—all basic block-and-tackle skills that aren't common for most small, local craft breweries. My risk was my ignorance of the craft-beer world, which I addressed by recruiting and working with great, experienced hands who would accelerate my own craft-beer education. Working with true craftsmen to execute the mission is a great joy to me, professionally and personally.

My wife and children supported my career change completely, and so did my friends. They can sense my energy for this new venture and comment on how much more I smile these days.

Some friends were nervous about my opening up a restaurant, asking, "Do you really have to do that? Take on more risk? Use so much capital for bricks and mortar?" All legitimate questions. Given my experience, I understood the stakes, and my caution prompted me to set the bar even higher to justify launching the business.

GETTING A *BLAZERECHTOMY*

To prepare for the transition from the venture-capital to the craft-beer community, I had to go to a specialist to have a procedure called a *blazerechtomy*. The process involves peeling off the blue blazer you've been wearing for twenty-five years and trading your khakis for a pair of blue jeans. I'm happy to say the procedure was a complete success.

When I first started Forbidden Root, it was clear that there were people who profiled me as a slick, private-equity Manhattanite. Part of what attracted me to craft beer, though, was the level playing field. It's the ultimate meritocracy. There's no terroir, grapes, bugs, or weather to affect the outcome of "the liquid." Either it's great or it isn't. Each brewery buys grain, yeast, and hops from similar sources. While expensive equipment can make your process more efficient and affect flavor somewhat, good brewers know their equipment and can control the recipe, time, and temperature to get their desired results.

Ultimately, the liquid you brew is who you are. It's as pure an investment of love and passion—other than parenting—that I've ever seen, and it's in as fair-minded and warm a community as I have ever had the privilege to be a part of.

A Search for Authenticity

In the wake of the 2007 financial collapse, our culture has been shifting. Issues of accountability, supply-channel integrity, and food sourcing are all interrelated. Many people today are questioning their goals and searching for their own true north. After years in an increasingly corporate industry, I felt the same.

Craft-beer culture fulfills many needs for me; it's all about collaboration, supporting the community, pushing boundaries, and being down-to-earth. There's an emphasis on creativity. The environment is full of characters, with plenty of room for obsessives like me, who, at 2:00 a.m., are seeking the best source of dried fig leaves.

Forbidden Root is a benefit corporation, which means we're committed to doing good as well as making money. One hundred percent of the profits from our nonconsumable sales of apparel, glasses, and such, go to charity. Knowing that we're supporting the larger community while doing something we love is extremely gratifying.

From Root Beer to a Restaurant

Once Randy and I had decided to move forward with Forbidden Root, we spent six months researching and another two years trying out our products on an increasingly larger market. Randy, BJ, and I made test batches with a pilot station we had bought, in a garage we rented, and scaled up from there to pour at local festivals.

I quickly learned how to show up to a liquor store, improvise a table, score some ice, and create a set-up for sampling our beer. I learned how to describe a beer in five, thirty, or sixty seconds, depending on the level of a consumer's interest. It's a combination of entertainment, romance, and education, but it's mostly about connection—connection to people, to our brand, to the soil, and to the history and spirit of our ancestors, who brewed what they could forage locally.

As Forbidden Root continued to grow in its early years, I understood that we needed to open a restaurant and brewery where people could taste our beers and experience our brand. I never thought I would open a restaurant, which takes a monumental amount of time, effort, and capital. Looking back, though, I know we made the right choice.

Welcome to the Neighborhood

Our brewery and restaurant is in a landmark building that used to be The Hub, one of Chicago's grand movie theaters. The theater's old projection room is now my rootmaster area, where I tinker with elixirs and extracts.

When you walk into the pub, antique John Deere cultivator wheels hung from the ceiling subtly point out the relationship of our food and beers to those who till the soil. In addition to our commitment to natural ingredients, we're also committed to fostering social interaction. Our beer comes to the bar along a rail system over the bar, positioning the taps out of the line of sight of seated customers. We are the antisports bar, with no shiny objects to distract from focusing on good friends, good beer, and good food (although we do have two great TVs behind the beer boards, which will open when a Chicago team is in the playoffs).

One of the most humbling parts of this experience is the outpouring of support we've received from the neighborhood. The property needed to be rezoned, so we had to convince our alderman that Forbidden Root would be a good addition to West Town. We worked with the West Town Chamber of Commerce to develop a survey and hosted a community night at the bar to gauge public opinion.

> **One of the most humbling parts of this experience is the outpouring of support we've received from the neighborhood.**

The night of our community event was bitterly cold and windy. Usually, this type of event draws forty or fifty people, but we were sure no one would brave the frigid weather. We were wrong because 334 people showed up. They filled out surveys asking whether the city should allow us to open. Six said no, twelve responded maybe, and 284 said yes before we ran out of ballots. That's when we knew we were here to stay.

Not Your Grandma's Perfume

Forbidden Root's beers are now distributed in Illinois, New York, Massachusetts, and Rhode Island, and are available in over two hundred local bars, restaurants, and points of retail. As we continue to expand our reach, the restaurant and brewery serve as our showcase and innovation flywheel. Our customers tell us what they love and what could be better, and we use that feedback to refine our recipes.

We have twelve taps for our own beers and four guest taps, including a permanent "love handle," which we operate in partnership with another brewery, jointly picking a charity to donate two dollars per glass drawn.

When people visit Forbidden Root, they realize that botanicals are not your grandma's perfume. The more you get to know these ingredients and flavors, the more you respect them and use restraint when infusing them. The restaurant has been key to communicating our brand to people. When our customers visit, they really get our mission.

Who and What's in the Mirror

For those considering a career change of their own, I recommend doing some psychological testing. Trying to question yourself is a tough process. No one can objectively see who and what's in the mirror.

I was convinced that I was a contrarian because I often approached problem solving and product innovation differently from the way others did. I was toasted at my wedding twenty-five years ago as "an island," as my friend welcomed my bride to my island. But after going through some testing, I had an epiphany: I'm a people pleaser. Perhaps I gain energy by pleasing in a different way, but the core driver is adding value to a social experience. Although I didn't realize it then, not being able to please people in venture capital went against my natural grain.

Defining Yourself

Whether you change careers or confirm you are where you should be, questioning your achievements, your goals, and your potential future regrets is a great way to test whether you are your happiest, most fulfilled, most valuable self.

I think questioning your idols and benchmarking yourself against your heroes is an interesting exercise because it tests your open-mindedness to new truths. The one hero who stands the test of time is Muhammad Ali. He stayed true to himself, was extremely kind (to those outside the ring), set an example of what he thought was right, and radiated positive energy. I know I can't float like a butterfly and sting like a bee, but perhaps I can blaze a worthy trail.

I used my new gig to redefine myself as the rootmaster. I'm the only rootmaster, and I smile every time I see my title on my business card. It's a tiny but real reminder that I alone have the power to define myself.

Many people aspire to march to the beat of their own drum, but Robert has had the courage to actually do it. He left behind a highly successful investment career to pursue a path that may not offer the same financial rewards but comes with some pretty big personal ones. Being surrounded by high-quality beers and delicious food all the time doesn't hurt, either!

I also admire Robert's commitment to doing good, not just making money. The success of Forbidden Root has been a great thing not only for Robert and his team but also for the neighborhood and the organizations he supports through generous donations. It is great to see him use his many years of experience with new and growing businesses too—but now for himself and his own goals.

The list of places Robert has traveled and his knowledge of different plants and flavors—all in search of the next great beer—is staggering. I can't wait to see where he goes next and to taste the fruits of his labor. I envision him as sort of the mad scientist of beer. Please be sure to visit the Forbidden Root Restaurant and Brewery in Chicago and say hello to the one and only rootmaster!

ABOUT THE FIRST-TIME AUTHOR

Mike Harris is a proven and prolific entrepreneur. He has started and led several companies, mostly in the consulting and recruiting industries. Mike is best known as the founder and former CEO of Jefferson Wells, which grew from zero to $132 million in annual sales in just five years before it was sold to the global, human-capital company Manpower in 2001. Jefferson Wells remains one of the best stories of start-up to exit in the history of Wisconsin.

Mike is the cofounder and current CEO of Patina Solutions. This company also appears headed for great success with its model of deploying executives with more than twenty-five years of experience to help companies manage a myriad of situations and projects. Patina has essentially created a new "gig-by-gig" way to work for folks who are used to typical, salaried, single-company employment. Patina helps people develop the ability to do a "work 180," and that was the inspiration for Mike to create the concept of the career 180 featured in this book.

In addition to leading Patina, Mike frequently advises entrepreneurs who seek his recommendations on raising capital, hiring key leaders, developing growth strategies, and just about everything else it takes to start and build a successful enterprise. Mike often says he has never met an idea or an entrepreneur he does not like.

A lifelong resident of Wisconsin, Mike has long been married to his wonderful wife, Peggy. They have three great kids—Ellen, Claire, and Sam—who all have different interests and pursuits. For fun, Mike enjoys tennis, hiking, auto racing, cooking, beer, biking, making and listening to music, and many other pursuits. Mike can be reached at mikeharris@patinasolutions.com.